KNITTING FOR BEGINNERS

A STEP BY STEP GUIDE ON HOW TO KNIT THE QUICK AND EASY WAY. MAKE SWEATERS, SOCKS, BLANKETS AND MANY OTHER PROJECTS IN A FEW DAYS (IMAGES AND STITCH PATTERNS INCLUDED)

CHARLOTTE MILLER

Copyright 2020 - All rights reserved.

The content contained within this book may not be reproduced, duplicated or transmitted without direct written permission from the author or the publisher.

Under no circumstances will any blame or legal responsibility be held against the publisher, or author, for any damages, reparation, or monetary loss due to the information contained within this book. Either directly or indirectly.

Legal Notice:

This book is copyright protected. This book is only for personal use. You cannot amend, distribute, sell, use, quote or paraphrase any part, or the content within this book, without the consent of the author or publisher.

Disclaimer Notice:

Please note the information contained within this document is for educational and entertainment purposes only. All effort has been executed to present accurate, up to date, and reliable, complete information. No warranties of any kind are declared or implied. Readers acknowledge that the author is not engaging in the rendering of legal, financial, medical or professional advice. The content within this book has been derived from various sources. Please consult a licensed professional before attempting any techniques outlined in this book.

By reading this document, the reader agrees that under no circumstances is the author responsible for any losses, direct or indirect, which are incurred as a result of the use of information contained within this document, including, but not limited to, - errors, omissions, or inaccuracies.

TABLE OF CONTENTS

INTRODUCTION 5

CHAPTER 1
Knitting Basics 11

CHAPTER 2
Knitting Gauge 21

CHAPTER 3
Knitting Supplies and Materials 33

CHAPTER 4
Yarn 49

CHAPTER 5
How to Hold Needles and Yarn and
Make Your 1st Knit Stitch 55

CHAPTER 6
Some Basic and Simple Knitting Stitch Patterns 67

CHAPTER 7
Knitting Techniques 75

CHAPTER 8
How to Knit a... 87

CHAPTER 9
Common Mistakes (and How to Avoid Them) 107

CHAPTER 10
How To Finish Your Knitted Pieces? 121

CONCLUSION 129

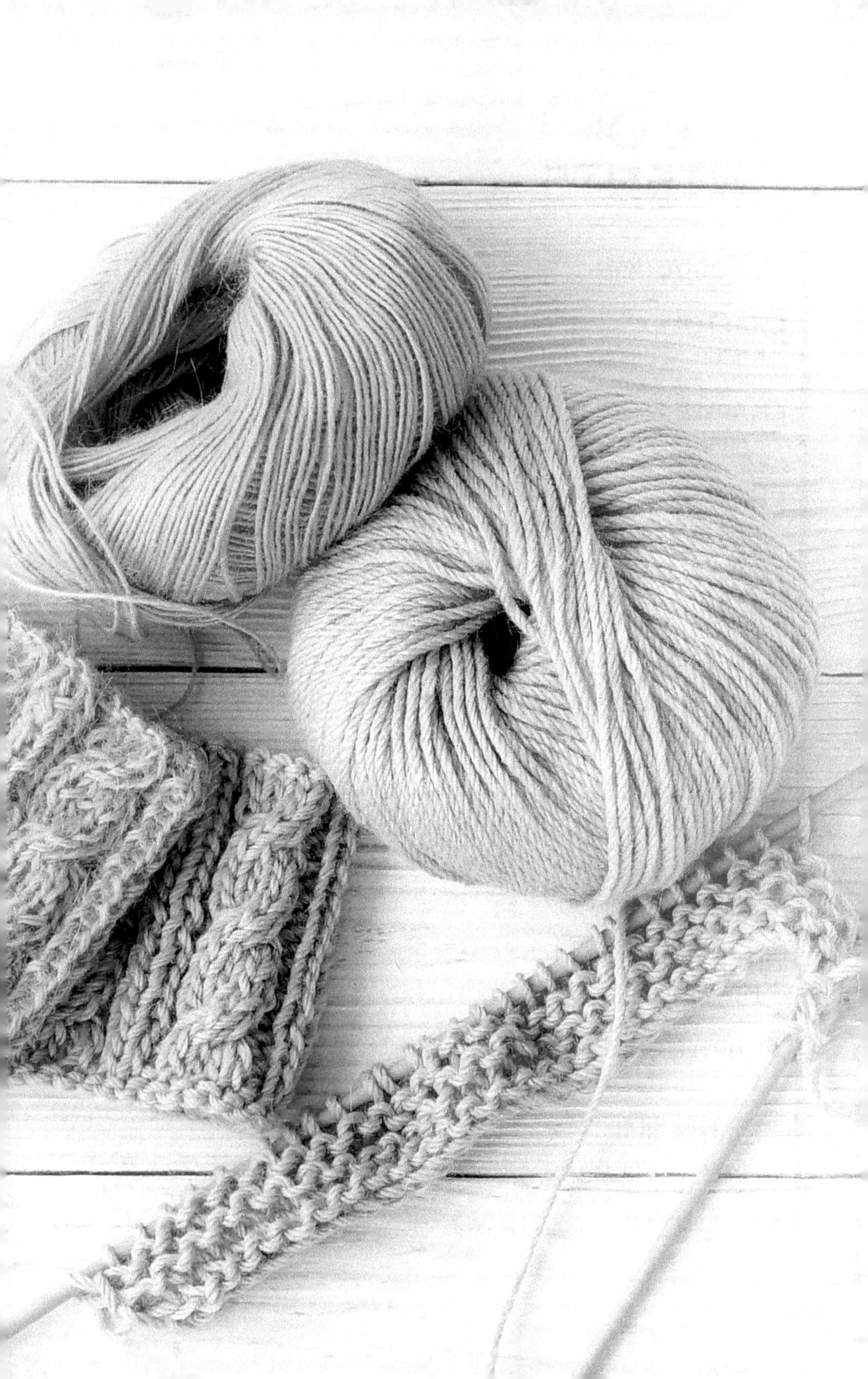

INTRODUCTION

Knitting is a strategy by which string or yarn is utilized to make a fabric. Sewn texture comprises of many back to back lines of circles, called lines. As each column advances, another circle is gotten through a current circle. The dynamic fastens hung on a needle until another circle can be gone through them. This procedure inevitably brings about a texture, frequently utilized for pieces of clothing. Knitting might be finished by hand or by machine. There exist various styles and strategies for hand knitting. Various kinds of yarns and needles might be utilized to accomplish plenty of weaved materials; these devices give the last piece an alternate shading, surface, weight, or potentially respectability. Different variables that influence the final product to incorporate the needle's shape, thickness, and flexibility, just as the yarn's fiber type, surface, and wind.

Knitting, creation of texture utilizes a constant yarn or set of yarns to shape a progression of interlocking circles. Sew textures can, by and large, be extended to a more prominent degree than woven sorts. The two fundamental kinds of weaves are the weft, or filling sews—including plain, rib, purl, example, and twofold sews—and the twist sews—including tricot, raschel, and Milanese. In knitting, a ridge is a segment of circles running the long way, comparing to the twist of woven texture; a course is a transverse column of circles, relating to the filling.

It doesn't require a lot of space as you'll need only a pair of needles and a yarn to build your art. It has been widely practiced nowadays as a type of therapeutic activity or as a hobby. Numerous knitting clubs and organizations such as Makers Mercantile and Ravelry are being set up to serve people in this form of art with passionate passion and enthusiasm. Some have still been questioning the legendary roots of the knitting art. No-one has ever known the exact date when a knitted object was first made. Knitting, however, is said to originate in the Middle East and is recognized among spinning and weaving as the youngest craft. The old knitted garments were made from natural fibers such as cotton, wool, and silk. These materials quickly decompose, which rendered tracking the period when this practice occurred even more difficult. We also mentioned the history of knitting in this article-from the ancient times to the present. So let's first find out and learn more about the wonders and mysteries in the world of knitting, before picking those yarns and needles.

In the fashion world, knitwear, such as sweaters and pullovers, played an essential part. It became a fashion statement for men and women of all ages and was synonymous with sports and leisure activities such as golf, tennis, and cricket. Even Coco Chanel promoted this craft and made widespread use of such objects and patterns. The popularity of knitting continued its trajectory on the great depression but altered its direction as a means of need. Since producing your garments was much cheaper, people preferred to make their own instead of purchasing the commercial products. In boycott British products, the people knead their clothes, demonstrating their self-reliance and freedom from the British. Martha Washington, the wife of George Washington, is a committed knitter too. She called the wives of the colonial army's high-ranking officials to knit and mend garments like socks and uniforms for the troops. Many cities, such as Nottingham, have become a leading producer of machine-knitted fabrics. Leicestershire's land and some of its neighboring countries have expanded into the hosiery or legwear market.

With the increasing number of demands on the market, the manufacturers of knitting machines have increased not only in production but also in the growth of the various types of machinery, such as the circular knitting machine. Knitting also helps with social interaction; knitting offers opportunities for people to socialize with others. Inviting friends to knit and talk with each other is several ways to increase social interaction with knitting. Even though they have never knitted before, it can be a fun way to interact with friends. Several public libraries and yarn shops host knitting groups where knitters can meet together to engage with other handcraft interested parties. Another exciting way that knitting will impact your life positively is to boost the flexibility in your hands and fingers. It keeps the fingers limber and may be of particular benefit to those with arthritis. Knitting can alleviate arthritis pain if it's a daily habit that people make. Knitting is no longer just a Grandmother.

Knit for Peace, an organization that brings together knitters to provide clothing for those in need around the world, published a literature review on knitting's health benefits. Our studies also have shown that knitting offers a wide range of health benefits. Knitting can produce feelings of relaxation and joy in people who regularly participate in the activity. Knitting reduces the average heart rate of 11 beats per minute, one, and results in lower blood pressure. This is part of the "relaxation response," which exercise such as yoga or jogging can also cause and create a similar meditative state. Knitting also helps participants to build community and interaction with others, resulting in a better mental state among those experiencing feelings of social isolation and loneliness. In cases where a knitter makes something for someone else, there's the extra gratification of realizing that they've helped someone else. Knitting's mental health advantages also continue to assist with the treatment of addictions. Creative activities like knitting help alleviate stress, which can help patients prevent a relapse. Chronic pain relief is another potential health advantage of knitting, possibly as a result of knitting that acts as a diversion and psychologically induces pain reduction. Knitting has been shown to decrease the chances of age-related mild cognitive impairment in terms of more comprehensive benefits to mental health. It can even help to alleviate dementia symptoms such as apathy and depression. With technology advancement, some computer programs have provided knitters with more comfort.

CHAPTER 1
Knitting Basics

Knitting is a process that involves turning wool or fiber into a fabric or textile by manipulating it in different ways to create a pattern. Sometimes knitting involves using two or more "needles," and in some instances, you can even use your hands or fingers. This eBook covers chunky wool knitting, and the only main differences are that:

- The wool is much larger and thicker
- The needles are much thicker and harder to manage

Something to note with chunky wool knitting is that it requires a great amount of upper body strength to hold the project, needles, and the yarn as it progresses and would therefore not suit those who lack this.

Benefits of Knitting

Certainly, knitting is fun and imaginative, but it can likewise lessen anxiety, kick-off proficiency, and change detainees. Studies demonstrate that knitting can even keep Alzheimer's under control! Who would've imagined this apparently harmless specialty additionally moonlights in wellbeing, instruction, and health? We should explore the advantages of knitting, might we?

As such, the system has been a reverberating accomplishment with an enthusiastic and developing hold up rundown. To date, more than 400 prisoners have experienced their week after week knitting class.

Knitting Helps You Overcome Addiction

The incongruity is that knitting itself is addictive, but the key is in swapping a really self-dangerous fixation for the moderately tame dependence of knitting. Knitting care groups like this one in Massachusetts and Australia's Knit to quit bunch for smokers have been transformative, to a great extent in light of the group bolster and knitting's innately relieving quality.

Knitting Encourages being social

Today, as in antiquated times, knitting is more social than any other time in recent memory, and everybody included appears to adore it. A study distributed by the British Journal of Occupational Therapy reports that knitters who are knitting much of the time are quiet, upbeat, and experience higher subjective working.

Understanding abbreviations & simbols

Alt - alternative

Approx - approximation

Beg - beginning

Wager - between

Bo - bind off

Cable - approach amount of stitch(es) as pointed out in style to the cable tv needle, hold cable television needle in leading of or back again of is indicated in structure and work following group of stitches per routine, then function stitch(es) from cable needle cc - contrasting color

ch - chain

cm - centimeter

cn - cable television needle

cont - continue

cross - shift amount of stitch(es) as pointed out in style to the wire needle, hold cable tv needle in leading of back again of is indicated in style and work upcoming group of stitches per routine, then job stitch(es) from cable needle dc - dual crochet

dec - decrease

dec(d) - decreased

dec(s) - decrease(s)

DP - dual pointed needles

DPN - dual pointed needles

foll - abide by, follows, following

g st - garter stitch

hdc - one half double crochet

in - inch

inc(d) – increased

inc(s) - increase(s), increasing

incl - including

k - knit

k1-b - knit one stitch in the row below

k1b-tbl - knit one stitch through the trunk loop

k1-f/b - knit another stitch but usually do not take away the stitch through the left needle, after that knit through the trunk loop of the same stitch and take away the stitch from your needle k1tbl - knit one stitch through the trunk loop

k2tog - knit two stitches together

k3tog - knit three stitches together

kfb - knit another stitch but usually do not take away the stitch in the left needle, then knit through the trunk loop of the same stitch and take away the stitch through the needle kfbf - knit another stitch but usually do not take away the stitch from left needle, next knit through the trunk loop of the same stitch and take away the stitch from needle kkyopsso - knit two stitches, create a yarn over, complete both knit stitches on the yarn over

k-p-k - knit another stitch but usually do not take away the stitch through the kept needle, purl through the trunk loop of the same stitch, knit into the same stitch and take away the stitch from your needle krb - knit within the row below

k-yo-k - knit another stitch but usually do not take away the stitch through the left needle, create a yarn over, then knit into the stitch once more and take away the stitch in the needle LH - remaining hand

lp(s) - loop(s)

lt - kept the twist

m - marker

mc - the major color

MK - help make knit

p - purl

p1-b - purl one stitch in the row below

p2sso - go two slipped stitches over the number of stitches indicated within the pattern

p2tog - purl two stitches together

p3tog - purl three stitches together

pat(s) - pattern(s)

pfb - purl into the front with the stitch but usually do not take away the stitch in the left needle, next purl through the trunk loop of the same stitch and take away the stitch through the needle pm - location marker

psso - forward slipped stitches over several stitches indicated within the pattern

rem - remaining

rep - repeat

rev - reverse

rev st st - opposite stockinette stitch

RH - appropriate hand

rnd - round

rpt - repeat

rs - correct side

rt - correct twist

s2kp2 - slide one stitch knitwise, slide one stitch knitwise, knit 1, go away two slipped stitches over the knitted stitch

sc - solo crochet

SK - skip

sk2p - slide one stitch knitwise, knit two stitches along, cross slipped stitch over

sk2psso - slide one stitch knit

skip - slide one stitch knit

SL - slip

SL st - slide the stitch

sl1k - slide one stitch knitwise

sl1p - slide 1 stitch purlwise

sm - slide marker

sp(s) - space(s)

ss - slide stitch

ssk - slide one stitch knitwise, slide one stitch knitwise, location kept needle through the front side of 2 stitches, knit two stitches collectively through back again loop ssp - slide one stitch knitwise, slide one stitch knitwise, cross the two stitches back again to the kept needle, purl the two stitches collectively through the trunk loops sssk - slide one stitch knitwise, slide one stitch knitwise, slide one stitch knitwise, knit the three stitches together

SSP - slide one stitch knitwise, slide one stitch knitwise, slide one stitch knitwise, cross the three stitches back again to the kept needle, purl the three stitches through the trunk loops st - stitch

t-ch - making chain

tog - together

tr - treble crochet stitch

w&t - cover and turn

wb - transfer yarn between your needles to the trunk of the task

wf - step yarn between your needles to leading of the task

wl bk - shift yarn between your needles to the trunk of the task

wl fwd - transfer yarn between your needles to leading of the task

wrn - cover yarn around the needle

ws - inappropriate side

YB - yarn in back

yd - yard

yf - yarn in front

yfon - yarn forwards and above the needle

yfrn - yarn onward and around needle

yfwd - transfer yarn between your needles to leading of the task

yo - yarn over

yo double - yarn over twice

yo2 - yarn over twice

yon - yarn over needle

yrn - circular yarn needle

CHAPTER 2
Knitting Gauge

In knitting, the tension, that is how tightly you knit, is a significant determinant of the design and characteristics of the finished product. In hand knitting mainly, the qualities of the knitter often influence the project. For instance, some people are nervous and tense, and their knitting is also tight and stiff. On the other hand, some people are relaxed and loose, and their knitting is also comfortable and free. Now, how does a pattern designer account for the tension of every knitter so that both the freest and tightest knitters can follow the same knitting instructions and end up with identical knitted material? The knitting gauge is the answer.

The knitting gauge is a measure of both the height and width of your stitches. It is usually expressed in two ways – rows per inch and stitches per inch. A typical gauge may look like this:

24 stitches & 32 rows / 6 inches in stockinette stitch, with gauge needle

The knitting gauge acts as a guideline for your knitting projects and ensures that your finished product looks exactly like the designer's product.

When do we need Knitting Gauge?

Knitting gauge is essential when you're knitting a project with a specific size — for example, sweaters, pairs of socks, hats, among others. However, if you are knitting items that don't require a particular size like scarves, you may not need to check the gauge.

I am sure that you will not like to get halfway through your project only to discover that it's going to be twice the intended size because you did not check your gauge before commencing the project. It is usually tempting to begin your project immediately, but it is always better to get the correct gauge before casting on. It will save you from tears and pain as you continue the project.

Knitting gauge is a function of three major things, which are yarn weight, needle size, and knitting tension. It might be challenging to change your knitting tension because it flows naturally from you. However, you can work around the yarn weight and the needle size to get an accurate gauge for your project.

How then do you Measure the Gauge?

The following steps are essential in measuring a knitting gauge for your project.

- Look out for the yarn type, needle size, and gauge on the pattern. More often than not, it is written at the beginning.

- Determine whether you need an accurate measurement for the kind of project you are working on. For example, a scarf will be exquisite even if it comes out a bit bigger or smaller than the instructions were followed to the letter. While other knitted fabrics like socks or hats have to be precise because they must fit on the user.

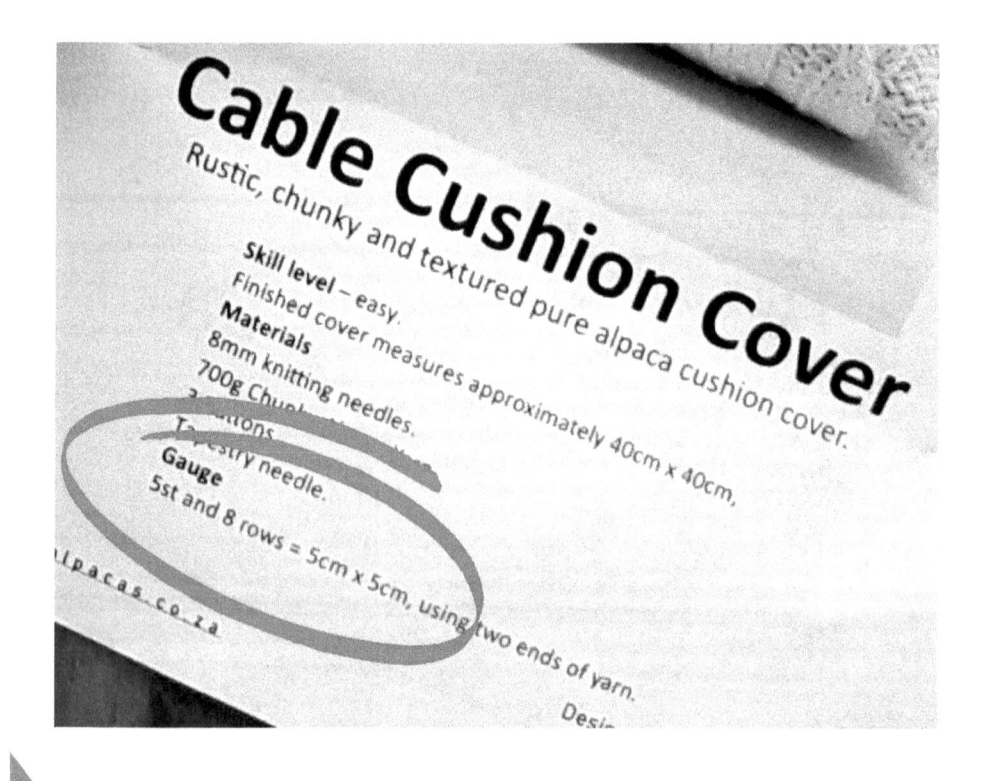

- Define the size of the swatch that will be ideal for measuring the knitting gauge. If you are working on a project that includes a leeway, you could use a 4-inch swatch. Otherwise, use a swatch that is between 6 and 8 inches.

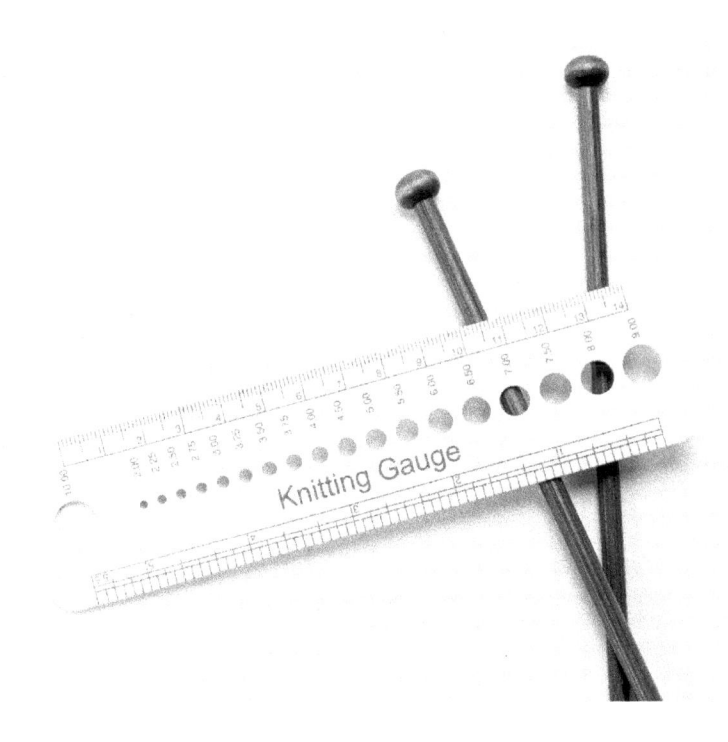

- Use stockinette stitch to knit the swatch. This implies that for two successive rows, you knit one and purl the other. You should always use stockinette stitch to knit swatches that you intend to use to measure the knitting gauge, except the pattern instruction states otherwise. If you are to make a swatch for a project with leeway (that is, a 4-inch swatch), you should use the recommended stitch according to the pattern instruction for the entire sample. As mentioned earlier, if the no-stitch style is recommended, use the stockinette stitch. However, if you are making a swatch for a project without leeway (that is, a 6 to 8 inches swatch), you should knit the first several rows of the swatch with a garter stitch until you have about 1-inch left for the border. When you have done this, begin and finish each subsequent row with about 1 inch of garter stitch. In the middle, knit with the stitch listed on the instruction or the stockinette stitch (if the no-stitch style is listed) until you are 1 inch before short of making a square. Then, finish the last inch in garter stitch. The border made with a garter stitch will mimic the amount of changes that will be made to the tension of the project, as well as help you to count and measure easily.

KNITTING FOR BEGINNERS

- Ensure that your sample lies on a flat surface. Set a hard ruler across the swatch, and count the number of stitches that are on every 4-inch of the swatch, but skip the edges. The vertical measurement will give you the rows per inch, while the horizontal measurement will give you the number of stitches per inch. To ensure accuracy, wash and dry your swatch before taking the measurements.

- Compare the pattern's gauge measurement to the measurement of your sample gauge. If your swatch is 1 stitch per inch more than the pattern, you can fix the error by making the swatch again with a larger knitting needle. However, if the stitch difference is more than 1, you should try making the swatch again with a thicker yarn. Furthermore, if the number of stitches on your swatch is 1 less than the number on the pattern per inch, re-make the swatch with a smaller knitting needle. However, if the difference between the number of the stitches on the pattern and the swatch is more than 1, make the swatch again with a thinner yarn.

- Ensure that you use the exact yarn and needles whose swatch gauge equals the pattern gauge for your knitting project.

CHAPTER 3
Knitting Supplies and Materials

Knitting is such an amazing skill to learn because it allows you to save a ton of money on clothing and the like, as you make your own textiles. Many skills allow you to save money doing your own projects, but they often require a fairly large initial investment.

Not so with knitting.

Knitting is doubly amazing because it is extremely cheap to get started. You can have a fully functioning knitting kit for less than $50. Of course, we must be clear here and realize that we're talking about knitting by hand. Purchasing a knitting machine will be more expensive, but we're not going to concern ourselves with machine knitting in this book. With a skill like this, it is always best to learn by hand.

Needles

It would be impossible to get into knitting without purchasing some needles. This shouldn't be a surprise, considering that knitting is a form of textile creation that is distinguished by the way you use two needles to create loops and stitches. They're pretty much as essential to knitting as the yarn is.

Yet there are forms of knitting that use neither needles nor yarn. These are much more unique forms of knitting and not at all what is meant when knitting is referenced in conversation or discussed online. So, for our purposes, needles are as important to knitting as breathing is to living.

That doesn't mean that every needle is made the same. There are actually three different types of knitting needles that we find most commonly used today. Are they the only types? Not even close. But beginners would do well to wrap their heads around the first three we're about to look at.

First, though, why should we use different types of needles? Aren't they just long sticks? Yeah, they are long sticks, but they are long sticks that have a distinct shape to them, which makes it easier or harder to work with certain designs. We pick the needle we use based on the project we're about to undertake.

Straight Needles:

Straight needles are the most common knitting needles. If you are looking to start knitting but don't want to invest in more than what is absolutely necessary, then you should start with a pair of these. They have a pointed end which is used for creating the stitches and a stopper at the other end so that your yarn doesn't slide off.

These needles are most often found around the 10 to 12-inch range, but they can be purchased in longer or shorter versions if you need to. They are made out of wood, steel, plastic, or bamboo most often, and these materials have their own positive and negative features, though many of these need to be discovered by the individual rather than being some sort of universal feature.

Straight needles are great for working on projects which are made flat such as washcloths. For projects that aren't going to be flat, they can be used to create the flat sections, which then get knit together to create the whole later on.

Circular Needles:

Circular needles are best used for round projects, as you probably guessed from the name. Instead of being a rigid stick, these needles are attached with a cord that can easily flex and be twisted into a circular shape. Both needles are connected together by this cord.

These needles come in a larger size, typically ranging from 16 inches to as long as 48 inches. They can also be purchased in different sizes, though their use begins to dramatically change as you play around with the size. The needles themselves tend to be of the same material as your straight needles, but the cord that connects them will be made out of nylon or a coated steel so that it holds onto the shape you twist it into.

You use these needles for projects that are round, like sweaters or hats. They can be used for flat projects, but you're better off sticking with straight needles when this is the case.

Double-Point Needles:

Double-point needles, often shortened to DPNs, are very short needles. They tend to average about six or seven inches in size, and they are typically sold in sets containing four or six of them. They get their name from the fact that they are pointed into needles on both ends rather than just one side.

These needles are used for smaller projects such as knitting socks. They are also commonly used in knitting toys or smaller projects which require a high level of control. However, they are among the harder needles to use, and so I recommend that beginners don't worry about them until they're proficiently using straight and circular needles.

Interchangeable Needles:

Interchangeable needles are a fantastic option for when you want a flexible needle with many different ways of using them. These needles are connected with a cord, but the pieces aren't stuck to the cord like they are with circular needles. Instead, these needles can be swapped out and replaced with different makes so that you can change the style, size, or length of your needles as you see fit.

In a lot of ways, this makes these less of a type of needle in and of themselves. They are more like a combination of the different needles we've looked at before. They offer the benefit of being able to switch out your needles, but you still need to know which needle is right for the job to make the best use of them. Once a beginner has an understanding of when to reach for a larger or smaller needle, they'll be ready to purchase and benefit from an interchangeable needle.

Cable Needles:

Cable needles are weird looking needles. They are pointed on both ends like a double-point needle is but the middle of the needle has an indentation which traps the yarn. These are used for knitting cables. You don't necessarily need to use a cable needle for knitting cables, but they definitely make it the best experience.

These needles are easy to differentiate from the others we've looked at, and I recommend that beginners ignore them until they are ready to start branching out into the world of cables.

Below is a small needle conversion chart to help you when you are purchasing needles so you can quickly determine if the needle will fit your project needs:

Metric/mm	US	Canadian/UK
2.0	0	14
2.25 or 2.5	1	13
2.75	2	12
3.0	XX	11
3.25	3	10
3.5	4	XX
3.75	5	9
4.0	6	8
4.5	7	7
5.0	8	6
5.5	9	5
6.0	10	4
6.5	10.5	3
7.0	10.75	2
7.5	XX	1
8.0	11	0

Scissors

Scissors are one of those tools that you probably already have, but if you don't, then you're definitely going to need some. Getting a pair of scissors that can easily cut through jumbo yarn will make your life easier since you won't need to worry about upgrading them down the road.

Scissors are used at the end of the project. When you finish your item, the yarn will still be attached to the ball from which it came. This is when we reach for our scissors and give the yarn a quick snip, leaving enough of a "tail" for us to work into the project. You will also find yourself reaching for the scissors when you want to switch colors during the project.

There isn't really much more that can be said about scissors. They just cut the yarn. But because they cut the yarn, you must aim to work with scissors that don't jam up or get caught when trying to cut fabric. Otherwise, they could damage the project. While chances are that they won't, there is a 100% chance that you'll get frustrated if they do. So purchase some quality scissors and save yourself a headache.

Tape Measure

A tape measure is always a useful tool. If you already have one, then you'll be fine. It doesn't matter if it is a tape measure for construction use or one that is designed for fabric use. As long as you can measure things, you'll be alright. With that said, it is worth noting that a tape measure that can be bent easily is always a plus, as it'll make measuring round objects a much easier task.

There are two key reasons why measuring tape is important. Pretend that you are looking to make a sweater, but you aren't sure what size it needs to be. The pattern you have specifies a size, but you're not sure if it will fit your intended recipient. You can use a tape measure to measure their dimensions, and then you can alter the pattern as needed for it to fit. If the pattern is laid out in stitches, then all you need to do is take the tape measure and find out the dimensions of each row of stitches. You can then use these to determine how many rows you need to remove or add to the project so that it fits.

The other reason that a tape measure is a must is that there are plenty of patterns that don't tell you how many rows to use. Instead, they tell you the size of the project in inches or centimeters. If you want to work on a pattern like this, then you need to be able to measure everything out properly, or you're going to find yourself having a frustrating time guessing whether or not you're doing it right.

Tapestry Needle

A tapestry needle looks just like a sewing needle, only it is quite large. The eye of the needle needs to be large enough to fit even the bulkiest of yarn. But unlike your knitting needles, you only need a single tapestry needle. You may decide to purchase a couple different sizes of tapestry needles, especially when working with lace or super fine yarn. Still, you only really need a single tapestry needle per size category.

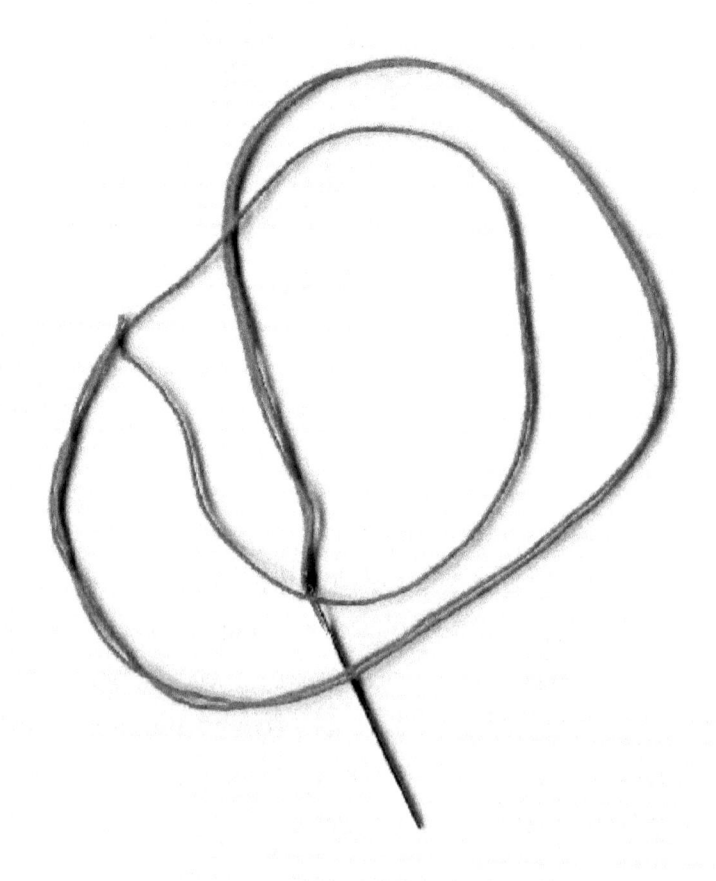

Remember how we mentioned leaving a "tail" behind when using our scissors to cut the yarn? This tail is what we need the tapestry needle for. We cut the yarn with a tail of roughly a foot long, and then we thread the tail through the tapestry needle. We then take the tapestry needle and use it to weave the tailback into the project. We do this with pretty much every project we'll make unless we happen to size the project perfectly to use every last piece of yarn in the ball.

Weaving the tail into the project in effect hides the "seams." If you let the tail just hang out of the project, then it would be clear where the project ended. It would also be much more likely that the tail gets caught on something and starts to unravel the project, which is pretty much the worst possible outcome we could have here. But when you weave the tail into the project, it hides where the project ends, and it prevents that ending piece from getting caught and pulling everything apart.

This makes a tapestry needle one of the key pieces of equipment you should purchase when first getting into knitting.

Stitch Markers

Stitch markers look almost exactly like a safety pin, only they tend to have a much brighter color so that they stand out easily. They're rounded so that they can easily slip over your needles as need be. Some stitch markers are designed to be slotted directly into or onto a stitch. As the name implies, their purpose is to mark your stitches.

Stitch markers can be extremely important, depending on what you are making. Simple designs won't see much of a use for these, though that doesn't mean they aren't helpful. If you start a row with one type of stitch before moving into another, then you may find it beneficial to use a stitch marker on that stitch, so you know exactly where it is when you start knitting the next row. When used in this manner, even on the easiest of projects, they can really help you avoid one of the biggest mistakes beginners make: shrinking or growing rows. But we'll talk more about this type of mistake in chapter six.

For the time being, I would recommend that you purchase some stitch markers. You should be able to get a dozen of them for a couple dollars, so they're only a drop in the bucket. Don't be afraid to use them, even on simple projects, if you feel like they could help. They're the type of gear that is used in a very personal manner. Your knitting needles are always used to make stitches. Still, your stitch makers could be used to represent a dozen different things, it all depends on how you choose to place them and what stitches you consider important enough to mark for an easier time remembering them.

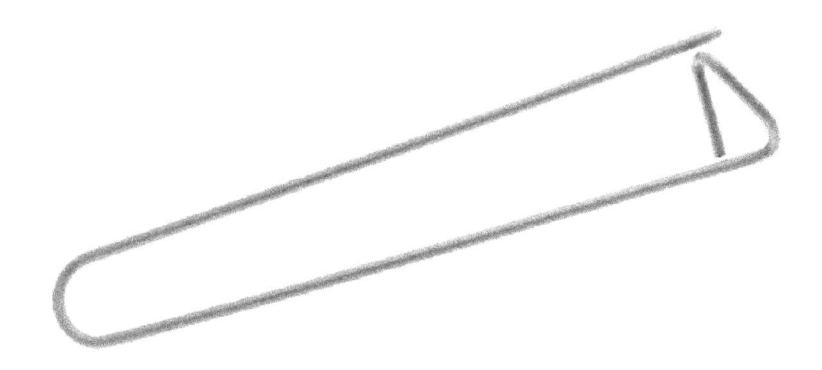

Stitch Holders

A stitch holder is like an even larger version of a stitch marker. They pretty much look the same since both of these pieces of equipment are designed based on safety pins. The goal of a stitch holder is to hold a stitch in place rather than just mark it.

With some projects you work on, you'll reach a point at which you need to leave some stitches out for later. For example, some sweater designs will have you work on the arm and then move outwards afterward. From the arm, the stitches move out in two directions, but we can only work in one direction at a time. In this case, what we do is we use a stitch holder to hold onto the stitches we're not using so that we can come back to them later.

Stitch holders are super useful tools, but they're not as commonly used as stitch markers. Nor are they overly common in patterns designed for beginners. They are quite cheap, however, and you may be interested in picking up a handful of them while making your initial knitting gear purchase. But if you can't, don't worry. You can always hold off purchasing them until you encounter a pattern that needs them. Just remember to fully read your patterns before you start working on them. That way, you don't get to the point where you need a stitch holder before you've had a chance to purchase one.

CHAPTER 4
Yarn

It's pretty hard to knit without some yarn. Not impossible, however, as there are types of knitting which use recycled t-shirts, leather or even glass. But 99% of the knitting you'll encounter out in the world, and 100% of the knitting we're looking at in this book, use yarn.

Yarn is the term we use to refer to any type of thread that has been spun for the purpose of textile work, such as knitting, sewing, weaving, or crocheting. Many beginners think that yarn is some special type of fabric, but the truth is that yarn can be made out of pretty much any fiber. You could use cotton from plants or the wool from a sheep. The fiber is spun to create a thread, and it is then bundled together into balls, which is the state you will most often find it in when purchasing for yourself.

Yarn can come in many different styles. The common defining features of yarn are color, fiber type, and weight. Color is a purely aesthetic choice, and it doesn't have an effect on the act of knitting, only on the way the project ends up looking. Switching fibers will have a major difference on whatever you are knitting. Some fibers are more flexible than others; some are more heat resistant than others; there are all sorts of differences that arise from changing the fiber you are working with, but more often, this difference is most noticeable on the end project rather than in the act of knitting itself.

As far as directly affecting the knitting process, the weight of the yarn is going to be a crucial factor. The heavy yarn is going to need to be worked differently than a yarn of a lighter weight. This will also directly affect the way that the needles you are using feel. You may find that you need to change the size of your needles to better use heavier or lighter yarn. This is where discussions of gauge come into play.

Most patterns will tell you what type of yarn they are designed for. These tend to use a numeric system with each weight assigned a different number. These range from 0 to 7, or lightest to heaviest. These cover: Lace (0); Superfine (1); Fine (2); Light (3); Medium (4); Bulky (5); Super Bulky (6); and Jumbo (7).

For anyone that is set to explore the world of knitting, you must know the needed materials and textures to achieve your desired result.

The yarn is usually considered as the main ingredient for every knitting work. Your choice of yarn for your first project should depend on the project. As you choose a project to be worked on, you must answer these few questions:

- What weight of yarn would I need?
- What quantity of yarn would I need?
- Would I need a novelty or basic yarn?
- Am I interested in a particular fiber?

So, after getting an idea of what you need for your project, you visit your local craft shop. You can browse through the various yarns that fit the needs you identified earlier and made your selection.

A ball of Yarn is an important tool to be used; it is a continuous thread of twisted fiber. Fiber can also be anything that can be gotten from natural wool or cotton-like cashmere, silk, and linen. There are some unusual fibers like bamboo; they can be synthesized to produce fibers such as nylon and acrylic. For some fabric, It might be challenging to find a suitable choice of yarn to use, but it is advised that you visit a nearby shop to learn more about yarn. But with a few guidelines which have been spelled out in this book, you should be able to decide on the suitable fabric to use. When choosing a yarn to use, be on the lookout for one that feels soft and smooth, and you could choose any color of your choice. When choosing the yarn, you have to consider the weight (thickness) and the size of the stitch.

The size of the stitch that yarn makes is usually referred to as the gauge or tension. When you get to a local yarn shop, you could get confused, even an expert in knitting may not be left out. So, at this stage, it is advised to stick with a yarn whose gauge is within the bracket of 16 – 20 over 4 inches (10cm). This type of yarn is more comfortable to catch up with mistakes, and it knits up faster than any yarn.

The second thing to watch out for is the blend of fiber. A yarn made wholly or partially of wool is advisable for use for any beginner. For instance, wool is suitable because it is soft and smooth, and when used for knitting, it is always impeccable and attractive. Wool is of different types of examples are lambswool, superwash, Marino, etc.

Various yarn textures

Wool

This is a textile fiber gotten from animal skin like sheep, cow, goat, etc.. It consists of protein and lipids. Wools are warm and soft. They are suitable for cardigan, scarf, head warmer, etc., especially for winter.

Cotton

Cotton is gotten from a flowering plant called Gossypium in the mallow family. the fiber is pure cellulose which is soft and fluffy

Acrylic

Acrylic is synthetic fibers formed from polymers. It contains at least 85% of the acrylonitrile monomer. It is a petroleum product which is easy to wash also it is lightweight and warm, etc.

CHAPTER 5

How to Hold Needles and Yarn and Make Your 1st Knit Stitch

There are different ways to hold the needles and yarn, and there is no right method since it will be the one that is most comfortable for you. The yarn can be held in both the right and the left hand, the needles can be held above or below.

Try both styles, they will be uncomfortable and slow at the beginning, but you have to keep trying until you discover which weaves more simply and naturally. The best style will be the one that suits you best and with which you enjoy knitting.

Hold Needles and Yarn with English style

(The thread in the right hand):

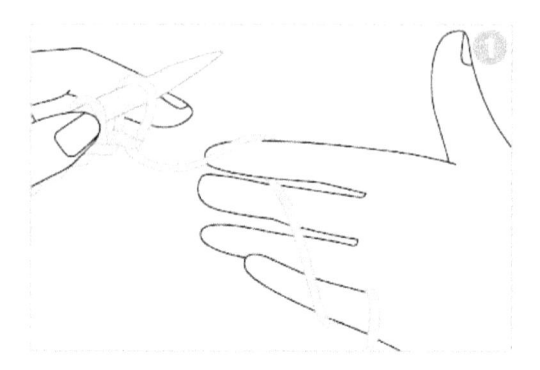

1. Begin by placing the thread in the fingers: wrap the pinky finger with the thread, then pass it under the two middle fingers and finally over the index finger of the right hand.

2. With the needle of the points already mounted in the left hand, grasp the empty needle with the right hand while the yarn of the ball is intertwined in the fingers to maintain tension.

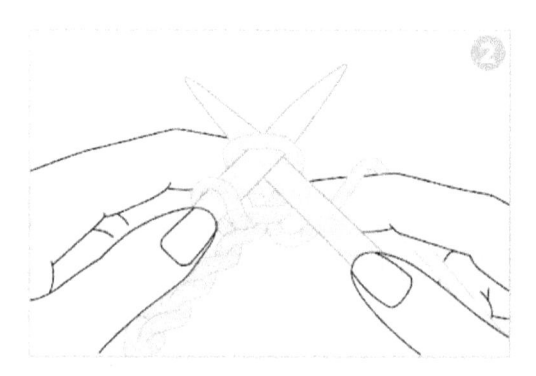

Knitting with Continental Style

The Continental style, also known as the German-style, is the most popular weaving method in Northern and Eastern Europe. When weaving with this style, the lacing of the way it is done with the English style is not performed. In this case, it is used to link the same needle and is passed through the point of the left needle. When doing this, a small movement is made with the right-hand needle. To weave with the Continental style, the yarn of the ball must be in the left hand. Advanced weavers prefer this style since it requires a smaller number of movements per point, and the right hand never has to release its needle, resulting in a faster weaving method.

Hold Needles and Yarn with Continental style(the thread in the left hand):

1. Begin by placing the thread in the fingers: wrap the little finger with the thread, then pass it under the middle two fingers and finally over the index finger of the left hand.

2. With the needle of the points mounted on the right hand, pass it to the left hand, while the yarn of the ball is intertwined in the fingers to maintain tension. Grasp the empty needle with your right hand. Practice these steps, and you will soon weave rhythmically and evenly.

How to Pick Your Yarn

Even advanced knitters get flabbergasted with the selection of available yarn. There are just so many beautiful choices! There is always something new. You can fritter away days going through the different options, enjoying the textures and the colors. It can be overwhelming how many choices there are and a challenge picking just the right one for your project. The purpose of this is to help you gather your supplies, so here is where you will learn how to pick your yarn.

Choosing a basic, worsted wool yarn in a lighter color is excellent to learn on. Choose a medium yarn weight rather than thin or thick. Make sure the texture is smooth. This will be the easiest to learn and practice on. When purchasing from a commercial yarn or craft store, always read the label wrapped around the ball for more important details about the yarn you are considering. You may find that some will indicate that it is better for certain crafts than others.

Reading a yarn label can be a challenge for those that have never looked at one before. Below are some tips on how to decipher the yarn label code:

1. **The Largest Letters**—The letters or words are dominating the label is the name of the company.

2. **Net Weight**—This indicates the bulk of the yarn: light, medium, or bulky. Look for the number "4" on the label. This indicates it is medium. "0" is for lace, "1" and "2" are fine, and "3" is light. "5" and "6" are bulky, and "7" indicates a jumbo weight.

3. **Length**—This is the total amount of yarn you will get in a ball. Make sure to check that the length is equal to or more than the project you are planning. If it is not, you will need to pick up more balls.

4. **Color and Color Number**—Typically, there is a name given to the color. It can be generic like "Bright Red" or more creative like "Robin Red Breast." There is a more specific color number associated with the color like "A432." If you are purchasing more than one ball of yarn for a project, double-check that the color and color name are the same. The color may appear to be similar, but when you start to mix the two balls, you will notice any subtle differences. It is best to do a little check here to avoid a disaster later.

5. **Dye Lot**—Similar to checking the color name and number, this Dye Lot number indicates that the yarn was colored in the same batch. Again, this can slightly alter the color of the yarn even if they have the same color name and number. This will be listed as a simple combination of numbers like "567."

6. **Fiber Content**—This number and name will be given together. It will appear as a single fiber and percentage, such as "100% wool," or a combination of fibers and percentages, such as "50% acrylic, 50% wool." When beginning for many projects, stick to more natural fibers like wool and avoid acrylic because they will split and slip on your needles. Also, even though cotton is a natural fiber, it does not have much stretch and can be hard for a beginner to work with.

7. **Gauge and Laundry Symbols**—Sometimes, the care instructions will be given to you in words and sometimes in images only.

Not all companies provide all this information or in this way, but you will find a lot of it on most commercial yarns. Here is a sample yarn label for you to see some of the information described above:

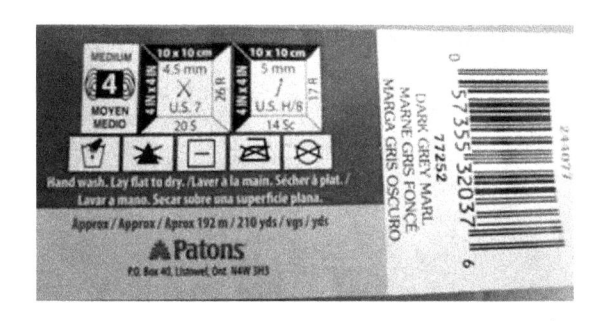

One key symbol provided that is especially important for all knitters, including the advanced ones, is with the crossed knitting needles. This is typically a rectangle or square with two knitting needles crossed inside and a lot of numbers and letters placed around it. This little box tells you what knitting gauge and needle size you need. The center where the needles are crossed has a number written above it, for example, "4.5 mm." This is what knitting needle size the company recommends for this yarn. Below this may be another number like "7 US," which indicates the US knitting needle size, in the event, you are shopping, and there is no millimeter measurement. To the left of the box are numbers such as "4X4 IN" and on top numbers such as "10X10 CM." This is information about the gauge swatch you need to make. It should be 4 inches wide and 4 inches long or 10 centimeters long and wide. The bottom of the box has a number and letter such as "20 S," and the right of the box has a number and letter such as "26 R." This information is about the stitches and rows. The bottom number and letter tell you that you should get 20 stitches ("S") and 26 rows ("R") into the 4-inch square. If there is another box next to it with a single hook, this is information for crocheting.

It is a good practice to save your yarn label with the swatch you created, so you remember all the information and have the care instructions. If you are giving the project as a gift, include the yarn label, so the recipient knows how to care for their new, beautiful present.

If you are not certain about the laundry symbols on the label, above is a cheat sheet to help you decipher the information:

How to Pick Your Needles

You may notice that there are hundreds of different options when it comes to knitting needles. They come in all sorts of sizes and materials. Some people swear by bamboo or wood needles, while others love metal, such as aluminum ones. Others enjoy the variety and economic benefits of plastic needles. As you continue practicing and trying out different tools, you will develop a preference, just like every knitter.

To begin, select a couple of different needles in different sizes to try out. Do not shy away from the curved, circular needles, either. These may end up being your best friend. Circular needles do allow you to knit flat and can actually hold a lot more stitches than flat needles. This is especially handy for large projects. Many knitters love working with wooden needles, especially in the beginning, because of the strength and slight give in the material. They also grip the yarn well, unlike smooth options like some plastics and most metals.

Just as suggested to start with medium yarn, start knitting with medium-sized needles. Check for sizes like 6 US, 7 US, or 8 US. If the needles do not have US sizes on them, choose 4 mm, 4.5 mm, or 5 mm. These are best for medium yarns and feel good in your hands. This also applies to the thickness of the needle. Thin needles are great for thinner yarn, while thicker needles complement a thick yarn better. If you have a medium-weight wool yarn, choose a needle with a medium thickness.

Another consideration is the needle length. This mainly applies to straight needles, but you will find the needles range in size from 7 inches up to 14 inches. Children typically use smaller needles, but you may like the shorter sizes in the beginning. Shorter needles can be less difficult to maneuver and easier to use. If a project is large, however, choose a longer needle so it can hold more stitches.

When you choose the pattern, you wish to knit and the yarn you will be using to complete the project, choose a needle that corresponds to the pattern instructions and wool label as described above. Do not attempt to knit with a different sized needle than the pattern and wool call for, especially if you are doing clothing. This will result in an ill-fitting final project and can be frustrating after all the time and effort you put into it. There is a huge difference between the needle sizes, so make sure it all matches before you begin your project. It takes some attention to the details, but it is worth it in the long run!

CHAPTER 6

Some Basic and Simple Knitting Stitch Patterns

Knit Stitch

Step 01

Hold the needle with the cast-on stitches in your left hand and the empty needle in your right hand.

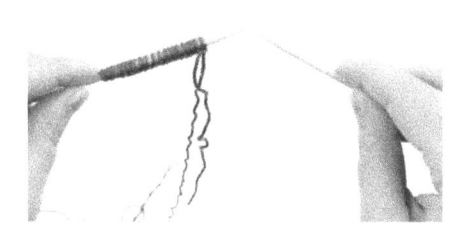

Step 02

Hold the empty Needle in front of everything in your right hand.

Hold the empty needle in front of the working yarn.

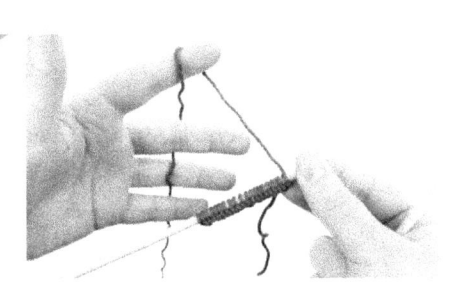

Step 03

Wrap the Yarn Around the Needle.

Wrap the working yarn around the new needle only in a counter-clockwise direction.

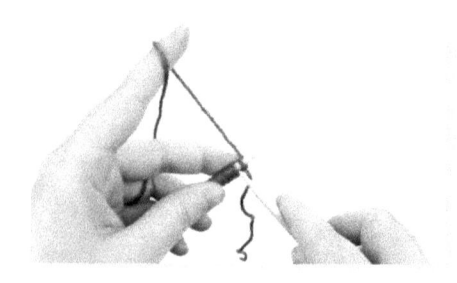

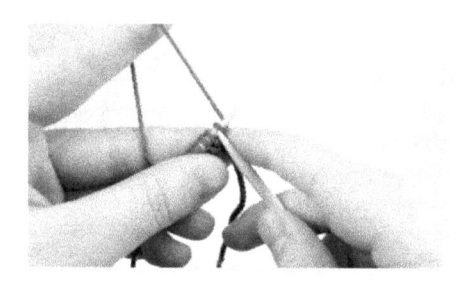

Step 04

Use the Right Needle to pull the Working yarn under the left needle through the stitch on that needle.

Descending the new needle down, cautiously catch this loop of yarn and pull it under the cast on stitch.

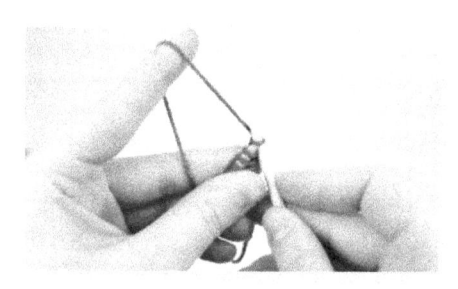

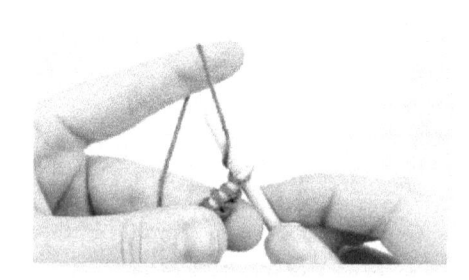

Step 05

Wrench the original stitch off of the left needle with the new stitch you just made

Jerk the remaining loop off the old needle, leaving the new loop on the needle that was beforehand empty.

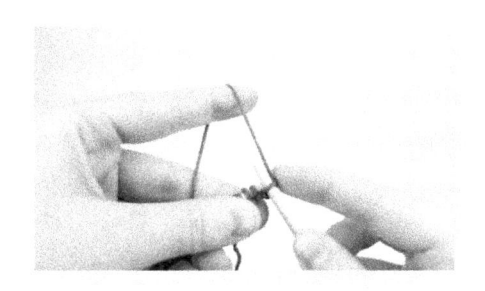

Step 06

Relapse Until End of Row

Reprise with all remaining stitches.

Step 07

Change hands after the last stitch

Step 08

Knit this row just like the last one.

When joining a row that will be all knit stitches, ensure that your working yarn is underneath both needles at all times.

The Purl Stitch

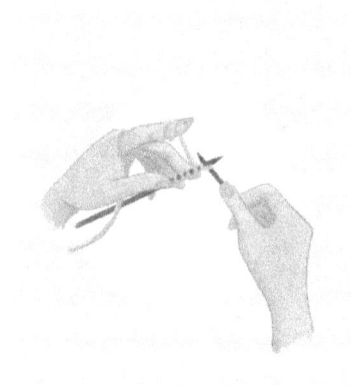

The purl stitch varies from the knit stitch in two important ways: The operational yarn is held in the front of the project instead of the back, and the needle is inserted from the back to the front instead of from front to back. Grasp the spike with cast-on stitches in your left hand.

- The garter stitch is usually made by making every row to be a knit row, the original row generally getting the ideal part.

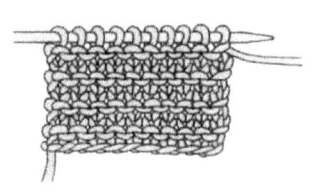

The same effect can likewise be arrived at by working every row as purl.

Equipping Stitch

Stocking stitch comprises one row of knit stitches honored by one row of purl stitches, and you start with a knit row that is the right facet of the work.

Reverse Stitch.

Reverse equipping stitch comprises one row of purl stitches adhered to by one row of knit stitches, beginning with a purl row, which is the appropriate side of the job.

Ribbing.

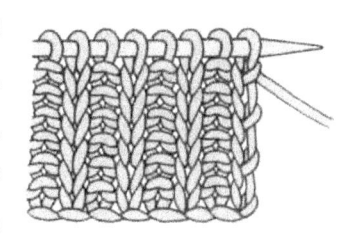

Ribbing is an elastic textile that is typically used for garment edgings. Both most normal kinds are 1x1 rib, which is developed by rotating one knit stitch and also one purl stitch and even 2x2 rib, which is formed by alternating two knit stitches and also two purl stitches. Care should be taken to purl the stitches which were weaved on the previous row and also vice versa.

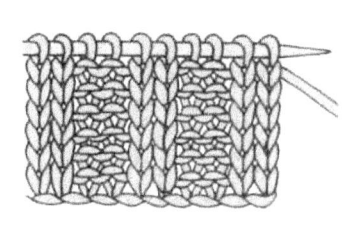

Knit One Below (K1B).

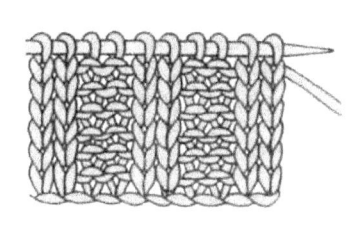

This stitch is in use in Fishermen's rib. Put the right-hand needle right into the next stitch, yet in the row listed below the stitch on the left-hand needle. Knit the stitch as usual.

How to Knit in the Round.

If you would certainly love to knit sleeves or socks, weaving in the round is an excellent ability to have. Determine if you wish to knit on round needles so you can quickly knit tubular shapes. If you like, you can make use of several dual pointed needles to knit in the round as well as form your material. Utilizing a magic loop technique is another prominent method to interweave in the circles using round needles considering that it's a fast way to knit several rows.

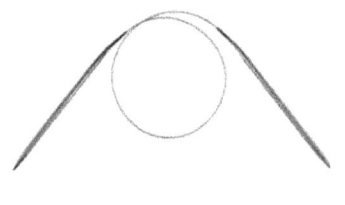

Cast your stitches onto a round needle. Select any round cord that you're comfortable with making use of as long as it's suitable for your task. Utilize a circular needle with a wire that's shorter than the diameter of what you're weaving. If you are knitting a jacket using a 34-inch (86-cm) diameter, start using a needle having a wire that's not more than 29 inches (76-cm) long. The team on as many stitches as you need for the knitting job.

You can get cables from 9 to 60-inches (22 centimeters to 1.5-meters) long.

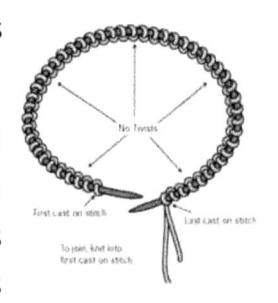

Glide the stitches onto the wire and needle along with the functioning yarn once you have cast on as many stitches as you need to maneuver the stitches down onto the cable connection. The sutures will be near the notion of the remaining needle.

Look for twisted stitches. Smooth the stitches, so they're facing similarly as well as aren't turned. The cast-on stitches shouldn't loophole or spin over the cord. It's vital to do this before you start weaving, or the fabric will undoubtedly have a warped shape that you can't undo later.

Place a stitch marker on your needle. As you prepare to start knitting, place a stitched pen on the very best pointer. The stitch pen will undoubtedly help you in monitoring the number of rows you've made.

You may get logical stitch markers at the craft shops, sewing retailers, and also some food markets.

Knit the first row. Place the right needle pointer into the stitch on the left needle. Cover the working yarn around the needle and also move the finished knit stitch onto the appropriate needle. Keep knitting up until you've knitted the whole row and also are back at the stitch marker.

Ensure that you're knitting with the functioning yarn and not the yarn tail.

Continue steadily to knit until you've arrived at the desired span. Maintain knitting every row until your textile options are as long as your pattern advises. Be aware that every time you attain the stitch pen, you've finished yet another row.

If you're working from a pattern, keep in mind that you're always working with the best side of the material.

CHAPTER 7
Knitting Techniques

English Style

Knitting in English-style is achieved by keeping the yarn in your right hand. The patterns are formed on the piece's exterior (public-facing) face. Knitting English style (also known as' throwing') is characterized by holding the yarn in your right hand and wrapping it around the needle. The movement can be subtle or deliberate, and there are countless variations of how your right-hand holds the yarn. English knitting is a knitting style that includes keeping the thread, alongside the working needle, in the dominant hand. While it is popular in the British Isles and North America, knitting in English is done worldwide by knitters and is perhaps the most common. More than 60 percent said they knit English style in a survey of just under 300 all Free Knitting writers.

Continental Style

Continental knitting is accomplished by holding both the knitting and the purling yarn in your left hand. The patterns are formed on the piece's exterior (public-) face. Continental knitting (also known as' picking') is reputed to be easy. The yarn is kept in your left hand, and you don't need to move the thread at all once you get used to this form. Only pick the pin and get on with it. Continental knitting is a type of knitting, where the knitter keeps the yarn with the non-dominant side. Most knitters find this approach much faster, and crochets who are learning how to knit also find continental in their hands feel more normal. Approximately 30 percent of knitters from the above survey knit continental. As this style keeps the material in the hand that is not dominant, to switch between knitting and purling, it is unnecessary to transfer the thread either in the front or in the back of the needles. Instead, the yarn is either positioned in the non-dominant hand above or below the needle.

Norwegian Knitting

The Norwegian knitting style is distinct due to the way purl stitches are handled. This particular hold places the working yarn in the non-dominant side, making it a continental variant; the knit stitches are worked much like the standard continental type.

Russian Knitting

Russian knitting is very similar to standard continental knitting, and the knit and purl stitches are worked in the same way themselves. The only difference with Russian knitting is that the working yarn is wrapped around the non-dominant hand's pointer finger, very similar to where it originates as the leading leg from the cloth. It makes a very close grip on the Russian style that helps you to flip the yarn over the tip of the needle instead of taking it with the needle itself. This technique is similar to kneading the lever with the yarn in the non-dominant hand.

Portuguese/ Incan/ Turkish Style

By holding the yarn around the neck or from a hook in the necklace type, this method is done, enabling the knitter to knit on the opposite. Usually, patterns are produced by stranding the yarn outside the piece. This knitting style is a real attention-getter— you tie the yarn to tension around your arm, and then just flip the working yarn to create stitches with your thumb. Purl stitches are usually quicker with this style, so it's perfect on the wrong side to work stockinette in the round. Portuguese knitting is a particularly great knitting keep since the yarn tension is not at all carried in the hands. Rather, Portuguese knitters tie the yarn around their necks. The rationale why numerous knitters like this style are because pace makes the fingers frees up. The tension is kept in the hands in every different knitting style; this provides two things for the hands to do at the same time— keep the yarn and work the stitches with the needles. There's one less thing you have to think about when making the stitches when the stress is kept around the arm. This technique is also perfect for helping with knitting discomfort since the yarn retains so much of the tension in the hands. If you're not into out of the way to knit with the yarn around your arm, you can also purchase a Portuguese pin that added to your shirt and keeps the tightness there.

Combination Knitting

Consider combination knitting if you are searching for ways to make your Continental knitting even quicker. To be more productive, the purl stitches are twisted the reverse way around, meaning the knit stitches are going around through the other loop.

The Slip Knot

Nearly all cast-ons require a slip knot. If you do not know how to make a slip knot, taking a few minutes to master this simple knot will help you moving forward.

- Make a loop in the yarn.
- Hold the loop between your right forefinger and thumb, where the yarn crosses.
- Make a second loop with your left hand.
- Feed the second loop through the back of the first and pull taut.

- Adjust your slip knot by pulling on the free end of the thread.

Casting On

The first step to knitting is called "casting on". This is done by creating the first row of stitches on your needle. This is your foundation and will become one side of your scarf, so it is important to make it neatly. There are many methods of casting on. Some types are more suitable for specific projects, but the long-tail cast-on is most common. You will never go wrong by mastering the long-tail cast-on technique!

In the example above, we determined that the 6-inch scarf requires a total of 24 stitches for the width. Start by measuring a piece of yarn. Allow 1 to 2 inches for each stitch you will be casting on. If you are using a Bulky or Chunky yarn and big needles, you will need 2 inches per stitch (48 inches, or 4 feet). If you are using a finer yarn and smaller needles, you will be fine with the 1-inch estimation. I usually add about 6 inches to my total, just to be safe.

Do not cut the yarn. Just hold it where you have measured your desired length.

Step 01

Make a slip knot at the place where you have marked the length of your yarn for casting on. Slip the loop over one needle and pull the tail to tighten it.

Step 02

Hold the needle in your right hand with your index finger on top, holding the slip knot in place.

Step 03

With your left hand under the needle, wrap one strand around your index finger and the other around your thumb. You should have a triangle shape with your needle at the top point and your two fingers, making the two points for the triangle base.

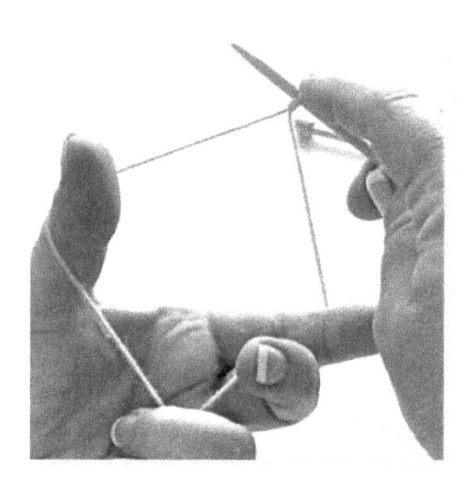

Step 04

Bring the needle down, so the yarn makes a "V" between your thumb and forefinger, which are now positioned like you are pointing a gun.

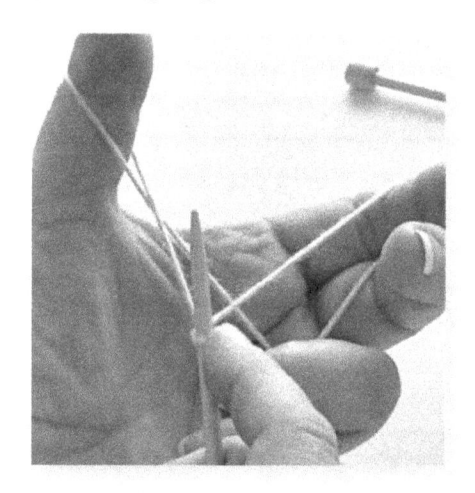

Step 05

With your right hand, guide the tip of the needle under the left side of the yarn that is looped around your thumb.

Step 06

Guide the needle UNDER this point and OVER the yarn on the right side of your thumb.

Step 07

Move the tip of the needle OVER the left side of the yarn on your index finger.

Step 08

Swing the needle back THROUGH the loop on your thumb.

Step 09

You will see that you have a loop on your needle now. Pull your needle up and release the yarn on your finger. Then pull the two yarn ends to tighten the cast on stitch.

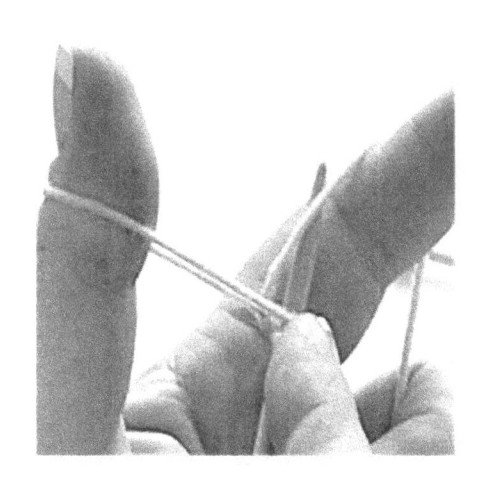

Basically, the cast follows this pattern: under your thumb, over your index finger, and back through the thumb loop. Use this as your Cast-on Mantra: Under-Over-Through, Under-Over-Through....

Congratulations! You have your first stitch. Personally, I think casting on is the most complicated part of knitting a scarf. Once you master this, the rest will be easy.

Knitted Cast On

Make a slip knot and leave it about an inch from the end of the needle. Slide your working/right needle into the slip knot from the left-hand front side and out through the right rear of the knot. Wrap the working yarn over the working needle counterclockwise (wrapping from the leftover the needle to the right). Carefully tilt your working needle to pull it and the loop that you made back through the original stitch.

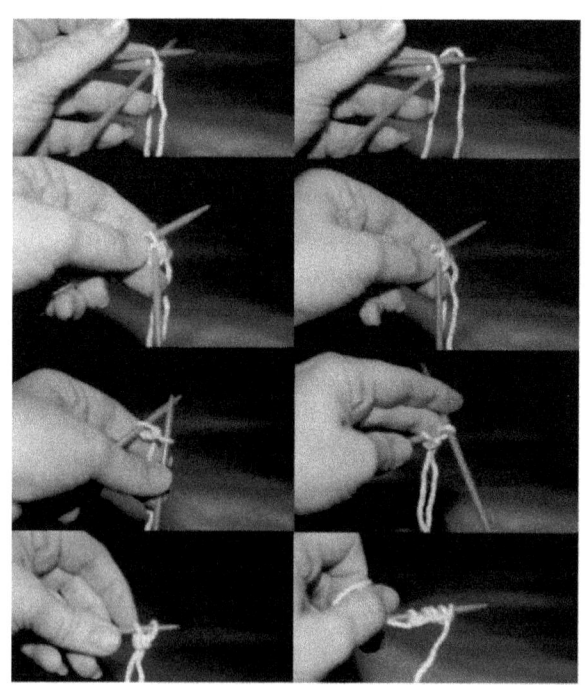

You will gently slide the new stitch onto the left needle by placing the left needle on the right side of the stitch and pulling it off the right needle. In other words, the left needle needs to go into the stitch from the same direction as the right needle did. Repeat this process until you have the proper amount of stitches on the needle.

Figure out How to Knit: The Long-Tail Cast-On

Figure out how to weave a long-tail cast-on making with this selective how to sew for tenderfoot's asset.

Making a long tail (around 2- and one-half inch" to three" for each line to be thrown on), make a slipknot and spot-on right needle.

Spot thumb and pointer of left hand between yarn closes with the goal that working yarn is around the forefinger, and the last part is around the thumb.

With your different fingers, secure the finishes a couple of crawls beneath the needles. Hold palm skywards, making a pattern V of a yarn.

Put the needle upward through the circle on the thumb, snatch the principal strand around the pointer with the needle, and return down through circle on the thumb.

Drop circle off the thumb and, putting thumb back in V setup, tenderly fix coming about join on the needle.

Be certain not to cast-on too firmly or freely — join ought to effectively slide to and from on the needle without looking free and "loopy."

Fledgling Knitting Practice: Cast on 20 lines. Presently remove the entirety of the join from the needle (I know, I know...) and cast on 20 lines once more. Rehash this procedure until you feel extremely great with this cast-on. At the point when you are simply figuring out how to sew, it requires a significant period to get that muscle memory instilled, so keep at it! It'll come, I guarantee.

If you are searching for help on the best way to begin knitting, this workshop is for you. With exercises intended for starting knitting needs, you'll get more than two hours of guidance covering lines, basic errors, and in any event, knitting in the round, yarn types, and completing methods.

Cable Cast-On

The cable cast-on begins like a knitted-on cast-on; however, after you make the first stitch, additional stitches are added between two stitches. The newly created stitch is moved to the left-hand needle and a new stitch made between this one and the preceding stitch. The cable cast-on creates a sturdy, reversible edge and is an acceptable replacement for either the long-tail cast-on or the knitted-on cast-on if you prefer it.

Knitting for left-handers

Don't be put off from knitting just because you are left-handed.

Instead of casting on to the left-hand needle, you cast on to the right-hand.

The needle you work with is the left-hand needle while the right-hand needle holds the stitches you're working into. Knitting and purling are the same concepts, where you still either work with the yarn behind your needle or in front of it. Your right side and wrong side of the fabric are still the same based on where those yarn bumps belong. A left-handed knitter just has to figure out how to make all of these basics feel natural without as much guidance as a right-handed knitter would find. Many left-handed knitters find that working in a mirror is great practice and helps them figure out the best ways to work.

CHAPTER 8

How to Knit a…

Blanket and Baby blanket

Difficulty: Beginner – the pattern is reversible.

Size: 30 inches wide, 33 inches long.

Yarn: 5 balls of chunky yarn – size 5.

Needles: A circular needle, size 10.

Tools Required: Stitch markers, a large eye blunt needle.

Gauge Instructions: 12 stitches and 20 rows = 4 inches

Pattern: NB – the circular needle is used to accommodate a large number of stitches, so work back and forth as if working on straight needles

Cast on 90 stitches

For the first 6 rows, knit the seed stitch:

•For the first row knit one and purl one all the way across

•For the second row, purl the knit stitches and knit the purl stitches and repeat this 4 times

Row 7 – work the seed stitch over the first 5 stitches for the side border

Purl 16 stitches

Knit 16; purl 16 all the way across until the last 5 stitches

Work the seed stitch for the final 5 stitches

Row 8 – work in the seed stitch in the first and last 5 stitches, and knit across in between

Rows 9 to 160 – repeat rows 7 and 8

Row 161 to 166 – repeat instructions for the top 6 rows, making the seed stitch for the top border

Bind off and weave in the ends.

Scarf

Make a sampler scarf which has fastener stitch pushes on both start and end, and 2 to 4 stitches of a weave on either edge to make an outskirt of tie stitch. Attempt stockinet stitch with minor departure from seed stitch to make structures all through. On the off chance that you put a ribbing stitch in the center where the rear of the neck will be, it will be smaller than the remainder of the scarf. Authoritative off or pushing off to complete your scarf. The following are a few investigations utilizing weave and purl for plans.

1. Purl the first and keep going stitches on the principal push. On the second column P, the primary stitch, K the subsequent stitch, P until the second to last stitch (K) in the example since you are on 'an inappropriate' side. On the 'right' side, you will K3, then P1, K until four stitches stay, at that point P1, K3. Simply keep moving; you sew or purl in toward the inside on each column until they compromise. At that point, you begin going out with the plan until you get to the edge.

2. This is similar to an Argyle plan without the hues. You can utilize diagram paper to make your structures. On the off chance that you know your measurements, you will have the option to tell precisely what it will resemble. If your lines and stitches are not square, it will likely be somewhat twisted; more precious stone than square.

3. This is an examination where I made a precious stone with purl stitches.

4. The example above is done two by two, moving more than one stitch each time. The accompanying directions accept a 20-stitch wide example with 2 sew stitches on each side to

forestall twisting along the edges. There are 16 stitches in the example. 'K' is a weave, 'P' is purl.

Lines 10-13: Follow Rows 6-9. Rehash this the same number of times as you like.

The clear squares are purled on the 'right' half of the undertaking. On 'an inappropriate' side, you will weave the clear squares as opposed to purling them. Charts are regularly perused from the option to the left and the base up since you are knitting from the base up. Else you will have a topsy turvy structure. The concealed territory on the correct side is sewed, the clear is purled. On an inappropriate side, you will purl the concealed territory and knitting where the clear is.

If you are purling on push 2, you will begin the left half of line 2, and continue up the draft in a crisscross way. Notice that I obscured lines 6-9 a subsequent time so you can perceive how it rehashes. The highest point of the chart doesn't exactly go similar to the knitting in the photograph. At the point when you get to the highest point of the chart, and you need to proceed, return down to push 6 and rehash the columns 6 through 9 the same number of times as you like. With only a pencil and some chart paper, you can test diagramming your geometric plans. Make sure to peruse them from the option to left and start at the baseline and continue upwards. At the point when you are on an inappropriate side/purl side, you will follow the example from the left to one side. Your knitting goes to and for, as a crisscross, that is how you'll follow the diagram. Indeed, when you backpedal on the even lines, on the purl side, you will purl the dull squares and sew the clear squares.

If you are knitting in the round, which I put in a later exercise, you will begin at the base right and proceed up the diagram moving from the correct side to one side. Now you are knitting to and for, so you will sew from the privilege to one side on odd columns, from the left to one side on even lines, in a crisscross design.

Hat

Needles—US 9- or 5.5-mm Yan Weight—4, medium weight, about 100 yards for sewing closed

Gauge:

Gauge—16-20 S (stitches) in 4 inches

1. Cast on 74 stitches.
2. Knit a 1 x 1 ribbed knit, knit one, and purl one for 6 rows.
3. Move to a stocking stitch, knitting one full row and t hen purling one full row until the total length is 7 inches, or 18 centimeters, from the casted edge to the end that is a purled row.

4. On the following row, knit two together across for 37 stitches.
5. Purl one full row.
6. Knit two together across a full row ending in 1 knit stitch for 19 stitches.
7. Cut 12 inches, or 30 centimeters, of yarn and thread it through a yarn needle.
8. Gently pull the final row of stitching from the needle and move the yarn needle through each stitch, pulling slightly to tighten and then whipstitch the seam together.
9. Add a flourish on the top, like a pom-pom or a flower to the side if you want. You did it!

Sock

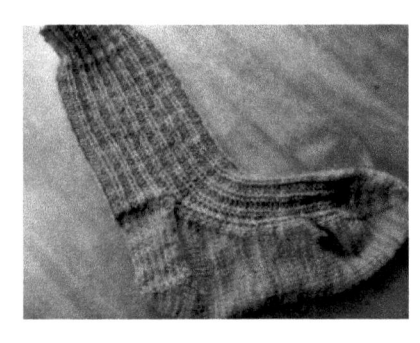

Provisions:

Needles: US 1 or 2.5 mm recommended, double round Stitch

Yarn: light, fried, about 420 meters or about 3 balls

Additionally: stitch markers, heel reinforcement:

Gauge - 32 S by 4 inches with sock seams Instructions:

KNITTING FOR BEGINNERS

1. **Create a bracelet:**

   a. Cast on 64 stitches, knit in the round, and mark with one stitch to mark the beginning of the row.

   b. Work 1 stitch, knit 2, and knit 2. Repeat pattern 2 x 2 ribs (2 reverse stitches and 2 reverse stitches) until the last 3 stitches. Knit 2 and knit 1.

   c. Repeat step "b" until the task is 1.5 inches.

   d. To make sure it is in the other sock, write the number of turns with which the rib was made.

   e. Next row, make 1 stitch, 3 stitches, and repeat the pattern for the groove length.

   f. On the next row, drag 1, make 3 and replicate the design for the row's duration.

   g. Follow steps "e" and "f" alternately until the task measures 7 inches, finishing on the second row, step "f."

   h. Make sure it's in the other sock and note the number of sliding stitches.

2. **Create a heel flap:**

   a. Row 1: knit 16, knit 1, purl 1, and 31 stitches.

   b. Make sure all seams are on the needle before starting the next set.

   c. Row 2: pass 1 and work 1 stitch, repeating the pattern of the line.

d. Row 3: move 1 and flip 31.

   e. Other steps 'c' and' 16 times.

3. **Turn the heel:**

   a. Row 1 - Knit 1, make 18 stitches, pass, pass, sew, sew 1 stitch, and turn it.

   b. Row 2: knit 1, knit 7, knit 2, knit 1, and knit.

   c. Row 3 - slips 1, stitches 8, slip, slip, knit, sew 1, and knit.

   d. Repeat steps "a" to "c", adding 1 more stitch before each reduction until each stitch is knit. There are about 20 stitches on the needle.

4. **Create a sock:**

   a. Sew 20 stitches, collect and make 17 stitches. Place the sewing tag.

   b. Knit 1 stitch, 3 stitches, and repeat for 32 stitches.

   c. Selection and knitting 1. Place the sewing marker.

   d. Pick up and stitch 17 stitches in the reinforcement area.

   e. Sew 10 stitches in the middle of the heel.

5. **Create fittings:**

   a. Row 1: Make-up to 3 stitches on the seam marker, then knit 2 simultaneously, make 1 and slip the marker. Start repeating Stitch 1 and flip 3 for the next 33 Stitch s. Move the pen and do 1, slide, slide, knit, and then do the rest of the row.

b. Row 2: Knit to the first seam marker and move marker. Start repeating stitch 1, mix 3 for the next 31 stitches, move the pen and knit until the end of the row.

c. Follow steps "a" and "b" alternately until you reach 32 Stitch s for the model. That's a total of 63 Stitch s.

d. Continue working, forming up to about 2.5 inches longer than the desired length.

6. **Create a finger**

    a. Start by knitting to the first marker and drag the marker. Repeat stitch 1, make 3 reverse stitches for 31 stitches, then sew 2 stitches together, slip marker and sew at the end of the row.

    b. On the next row, work 1 row.

7. **Create a finger shape**

    a. w. Row 1: work until there are 3 stitches left before the first marker. Knit 2 at the same time and knit 1. After moving the pen, make 1, slip, slip, knit, and knit within 3 stitches from the second marker. Knit 2 together, 1 stitch, slip marker, 1 stitch, slip, slip, knit, and finish the row. Yes.

    b. Row 2: do the whole row.

c. Repeat step "a" 4 more times, decreasing each time until there are 16 stitches left.

d. Tie a knot in the first marker, changing the seams on the needle so that the instep is on one needle and the template on the second needle.

e. Cut the yarn, leaving a 16-inch tail.

8. **Create/finish the sock**

    a. Using a sewing needle, sew on both sides with a stitch.

    b. Cut the ends and lock them in the design.

    c. Repeat for the other sock.

Sweater

If you need to knit a sweater, you need to realize how to knit an example of a sweater.

Before knitting the example, you have to know some fundamental advances:

Cast on

Here is the place knitting start, a cast-on is fundamentally made loops around the needle.

Knit columns

This is where the knitting venture begins getting shape, and knit lines comprise of framing the stitches.

Tie off

~The amazing finale! Official off is the last piece of a knitting venture, when the last column of your example is done, you should get your task away from the needles, and authoritative off is the system you use to do that.

Those are the three fundamental things you have to know, to finish any knitting venture.

Presently, about the materials to knit a sweater, you will require a Needle. You can't knit with your hands, what's more, more materials, for example,

Massive Yarn:

A yarn is that long constant string individual's use for knitting, crocheting, and sewing. Why utilize a massive Yarn? Since it is extraordinary for snappy projects and bigger projects where you need quick outcomes. The best piece of massive yarn is that it is anything but difficult to work with, which means it is ideal for learners.

Stitch Holders:

Stitch Holders are apparatuses that are utilized to hold open stitches, when not being utilized by the needles.

If you are knitting and you need to make an interruption and proceed with the task later, you need to utilize a stitch holder. Essentially this instrument is utilized to spare a venture for some other time. It is likewise valuable to recover needles that are being used if you need them for something different.

Stitch holders can be utilized when completing a side of the sweater and getting ready for the Kitchener stitch.

Stitch Markers:

Stitch markers are minimal round things that could be slipped onto the knitting needle to stamp a spot in succession. Stitch markers are ordinarily used to check the finish of a column in round knitting. They can likewise be utilized to check where builds, diminishes, or squares of various stitches ought to be set.

After you got all the materials, there are as yet one significant thing you have to know, and you need to acquaint yourself with any example narks, with switching back and forth among hues and conveying the yarns along as you are making the sweater.

Fringed Evening Wrap

Materials

- 4 -6 skeins of bulky weight yarn
- Arms
- Scissors

Directions

1. Cast on 10 stitches.
2. Knit 10-20 rows to make the shawl the length that you want.
3. Cast off.

To Make Fringe:

Cut 3 pieces of yarn that are about 16 inches long. Thread all three pieces together through one stitch at the end of the scarf. Double them and tie them in a large knot. Repeat that process in each stitch.

Bathing Suit Cover Up

Materials

- 4-6 skeins of bulky weight yarn
- Arms

Directions

1. Hold all the strands of yarn together and use them as if they were one strand. Cast on 30 stitches, or however many you need to make it long enough to go around your hips. Knit a row with a loose-knit stitch.

2. Knit another row with a loose-knit stitch. Knit the first two stitches together and continue knitting down the row until you get to the end. Knit the last two stitches together. Repeat for the next 10-12 rows, or however long you need to make the piece so that it reaches your ankles from your waist.

3. When it is long enough, knit the first two stitches of the next row together. Then knit the next two stitches together. And the next two. Until the row is finished. Cast off.

Thin Statement Scarf

Materials

- 2 skeins bulky weight yarn or 4 skeins of worsted weight yarn worked together
- Arms
- Tapestry needle

Directions

1. Cast on 6 stitches.
2. Knit 10-20 rows until the scarf measures the size you want. Cast off.
3. Use the tapestry needle and the tails of the yarn to sew the ends of the scarf together to make an infinity scarf.

Super Chunky Cowl

Materials

- 4 skeins of super bulky yarn
- Arms
- Tapestry needle

Directions

1. Work with all 4 strands of the super bulky yarn together as one strand to make a massive chunky strand. Cast on 6 stitches.
2. Work 10-12 knit rows until the cowl fits you.
3. Cast off. Fold the knitted piece in half and sew the ends together to make a cowl.

Simple Accent Scarf

Materials

- 5-10 skeins of worsted weight yarn
- Arms

Directions

1. Cast on 10 stitches.
2. Use I-Cord stitch to knit as many rows as you need to make the scarf about 50" long.
3. Cast off. Add fringe if you want to make it a little more dramatic.

Throw Rug

Materials

- 12 skeins of super bulky yarn in any color combination you like
- Arms
- Large tapestry needle

Directions

1. This rug is made of several squares sewn together. To make the basic square cast on 12 stitches. Knit 12 rows.

2. Cast off. Repeat this process to make as many squares as you need in the colors that you want to use.

3. Sew the squares together in any pattern you like to make a complete rug.

Knitting T-Shirt

A timeless T-shirt is always a good idea, yet there are times when life requires something merely a little, well, a lot more. Like a thousand factors of light, its white cotton core peeps out from the linen string that wraps around it. In this Bluegrass Blue shade, it's like wearing the gleaming sea!

If that's not enough to get you started, think about how little completing this gem needs. Just one joint, an awesome inside-out one, at the top of each shoulder as well as a pick up as well as bind off the surface for the neckline and also armholes. Summertime excellence!

PRODUCTS

4 (5, 6, 6, 7, 8) skeins of Lantern, 61% cotton as well as 39% bed linen. We used Bluegrass Blue.

You'll likewise need it.

US 7, 32-inch circular needles

United States 7, 24-inch circular needles

A US 8 double sharp needle

Two stitch markers

A cable stitch owner

Sew holders or scrap yarn

A-Cap Sleeve Pullover Pattern

EVALUATE

28 rows and 20 stitches = four inches in stockinette sew on smaller sized needles

SIZES

35 1/4 (39 1/4, 43 1/4, 47 1/4, 51 1/4, 55 1/4) inches

To fit actual chest area of 31-- 34 (35-- 38, 39-- 42, 43-- 46, 47-- 50, 51-- 54) inches, with approximately 1-- 4 inches of ease

Finished Chest Circumference: 35 1/4 (39 1/4, 43 1/4, 47 1/4, 51 1/4, 55 1/4) Inches

Finished measurement lengthwise From Shoulder To Back foot Edge: 25 (25, 1/2, 27 3/4, 28 1/2, 31 1/4, 31 1/2) inches

CHAPTER 9

Common Mistakes (and How to Avoid Them)

You know that no man is free from mistake. Making a mistake is a habit of humans. The man who does not mistake is either a devil or an angel. Whatever the level of a knitter, he/ she is prone to make a mistake. The expert knitters may also make mistakes very often. So, mistakes may happen with you too. But you will be glad to know that it's not a great problem if you know what mistakes may occur and their possible solutions. With this, I am going to tell you about the probable and most common mistakes of knitting so that you can find them easily. I am also going to discuss the step by step easy solutions of those mistakes. Please keep your eyes fixed here.

If you find a twisted stitch:

In case of knit side: When you wrap the yarn incorrectly, just the row, this mistake may happen. Stitch dropping is also another cause of such type of mistakes.

In case of purl side: The backward or twisted purl stitch looks somewhat different from the regular purl stitch. For such a case, the back loop of this stitch remains closer to the needle tip, comparing the front loop. You can correct this type of mistake by purling it just over the back loop.

If you find dropped stitch:

In case of knit side: A dropped stitch is seen very often in knitting cloth. If you trace out such a problem, you need to work on exactly at the place where you have found the dropping stitch. If this thing occurs in the case of one row just, then you can fix it easily. For correcting this mistake, you need to place your right-hand needle just through the stitch, which is dropped along with the loose stand, which is horizontally situated just behind the particular dropped stitch. Then fix it using the left-hand needle.

In case of purl side: If you find a dropped purl stitch in a single row, then you may try to fix it in this method. For this, you should work only on the stitch, which has dropped. At that time, you should ensure that the loose stand is laid just in front of the particular stitch, which is dropped. Then, as like the knit stitch fixing method, you need to insert your right or working needle through the dropped stitch. Now you need to lift the stitch, which is dropped with the help of your left needle. Now you must transfer your newly created purl to the left-hand needle again. For doing this, you need to place your left-hand needle through the stitch after slipping the right-hand needle from the stitch.

If you find a running stitch:

Do you know what the running stitch is? If you find more than one dropped stitch in more than a row, then you can consider it as running stitch. It is not such a tough job to correct this mistake. If you want to fix the mistake, you just need a crochet hook. Using the crochet hook in a very easy way, you can fix the running stitch.

If you find incomplete stitches:

If there exists any stitch where the yarn has held the needle but really not inserted into the loop for pulling stitch, then it is called incomplete stitch. For correcting the incomplete stitch, you just need to work on the particular incomplete stitch. You need to place your right or working needle into the incomplete stitch, which is held by the left-hand needle, and move it back and forth for fixing the error.

If you find an extra stitch:

You can find an extra or an extra stitch just at the edge of your stitched cloth. In general, the first stitch has just one loop, but when you bring your yarn back just over your needle top, then instead of one loop, you find two loops, which is the cause for generating the extra stitch mistake. If you want to avoid this type of mistake, you just need to be careful somewhat. You need to ensure that the yarn is kept under the needle, especially when you are taking it back for knitting the first stitch. Nothing is complex here. Just keep your yarn at the front side of your needle at the time of beginning the stitch. You need not do anything more.

Tips and tricks

You already know that you want to knit and your know-how. You even have some projects that you can start with, and some are harder than others. Of course, that doesn't mean you aren't still a little intimidated. It can be hard to jump right in there, and it can be frustrating if you're worrying about every little thing. This is dedicated to tips to help you succeed and feel a little more confident with your new-found skill.

Stick with Inexpensive Yarn

This may seem like a no-brainer, but it's something that you should really try out. When you go to pick up supplies, you may get overwhelmed by all of the choices.

Some of them are bound to be more expensive than others, and some are even harder to work with. Remember that inexpensive yarn, especially manmade yarn, is considered to be easy to work with, and so it should be picked up first.

Of course, another reason that you'd want to pick up inexpensive yarn at first is that the yarn will be wasted, and mistakes will be made. If you've already sunk a lot of money into a project and then just put a lot of time and effort into it as well, then you're going to feel like you've wasted a lot more. This could lead to you feeling discouraged, and that's the last thing you need if you want to become a knitting pro.

Keep Your Abbreviations Handy

However, when you start to work with other patterns, it's important to keep that abbreviation list on hand if you want to truly keep going. You aren't always going to want to stop, look for it, and then continue what you were doing all over again. Having it on hand makes it easy to glance over and start to memorize everything that's needed to go in an easy flowing manner.

Knit with Others

You may feel a little insecure about this tip at first because you're just beginning, but when you're sitting down to knit, it's best not to do it alone. This isn't true for everyone, but a lot of people find that it's a hobby that they'll keep for longer and excel at more if they have more people helping them along and encouraging them.

Knitting with a friend is a great bonding activity, and it allows you something to do when you run out of ideas or want a nice day or night in with someone that you care about. You can even bounce ideas off of each other and help when the other person is having trouble, making mistakes less likely to happen in the first place.

Get Decent Scissors

Once again, this may seem a little obvious, but you don't want to get the cheapest or oldest pair of scissors out there. You must get a decent pair of scissors that won't fray the yarn that you're working on. Some yarn can be broken or cut in this way without repercussion, but a good pair of scissors will often save you a lot of trouble later down the road.

Take it Easy

It's important not to want everything to work out too quickly. Even after you're done with these seven projects, you're still going to want to make sure that you stick with easier projects at first until you feel a little more confident. Otherwise, you may end up over your head with no one to turn to. Practicing your basics will pave the way for lot fancier projects down the road, which you'll then be able to complete with pure confidence.

Organize Your Supplies

You may not be the most well-organized person in the world, but there should be some organization to your supplies if you want to knit without any added frustration. Always having to look for something is sure to frustrate you, and it may cause you to give up on a project entirely. You'll want everything where it's easily found and accessible. Having a knitting bag or basket beside you when you start is always a good recommendation, and having an organized one will be even better. It'll even keep you from losing the things that you need to finish, saving you money on supplies in the long since you won't have to rebuy anything. It'll also save you time so that you'll be able to complete your projects in a much timelier manner.

Try your hand at making your own patterns

After you have made a few of the beginner patterns, you will notice that you can anticipate what the next step will be because it is always that way, or you just realize it makes sense. In this case, you are ready to try your hand at making your own pattern. The beauty of this challenge is that it saves you the hours of reading through patterns, trying to find just the right one to make what you want with the skills and materials that you have on hand. A simple process for creating your own pattern is outlined below for you:

1. Define the needles to be used in the project, ideally in both the US number and mm.
2. Determine the yarn weight and length needed for the project. If you are uncertain of the number of balls or yardage, just keep track as you go along what you use so you can record it later.
3. Measure the final size of the project. Make adjustments for larger sizes, if you want to get really fancy, otherwise just leave it at what you made 4. Gauge is sometimes important and sometimes not, depending on the project. As you knit, measure the stitches and rows in a 4-inch square. This is the gauge. Record this information. If the project is smaller, measure the stitches and rows in a 1-inch square.
4. If anything additional is needed to complete the pattern, like stitching markers, a yarn needle, or a fastener, make sure to write it down.
5. When you are writing the instructions—

    Begin with how many stitches to cast on.

    Try to be as clear and detailed as possible. Breaking it down by row is often the easiest method for presenting the steps.

    If your project is going to increase or decrease, make sure to be clear about how many stitches it will grow or shrink by.

Watch capitalization, punctuation, and abbreviations. Stay consistent and clear.

If the pattern is going to involve multiple steps or pieces, use headers that are clear and precise.

If working in the round, make sure to mention stitch markers if you want them to be used.

Always end the pattern with the bind off instructions and steps on how to complete the project. Sometimes, you will need to sew the project together or add a closure, so include instructions on these steps as well.

6. If you are introducing a new or complicated stitch to your pattern, add images or diagrams to help the knitter understand what to do.

7. If you want to show how to adjust sizing, include a schematic with the information.

Check out new and challenging stitches

In the previous projects, you were introduced to a few different stitches beyond the basics introduced in the very beginning. Just like you dove in and tackled those, now is the time to try your hand at even more advanced variations. Things like the "daisy" and "left twist" can sound scary, but when you break it down, you will see it is just another form of the basic knit, but it adds a new flair to an otherwise "basic" pattern. Think about the previous patterns in Chapters 3 and 4 and try replacing some of the stocking stitch rows with a few of these more intermediate stitches and watch how it completely transforms your project. Just this simple switch ramps up your project to an "intermediate" level but keeps the majority of the pattern the same, so you can create something you are more familiar with.

Just keep learning, just keep learning, just keep learning…

Take the time to celebrate your accomplishment of reaching this coveted intermediate status, but do not let yourself stay here forever. You have worked so hard to learn the skills necessary to get here. Keep challenging yourself to new projects. Consider projects with more pieces or steps that are made of all challenging stitches, or include materials that are not normally associated with knitting (think plastic or beads). What can it hurt to give it a go?

Keep your stuff where it belongs

If you do not have a place for all your knitting supplies, now is the time to find a storage solution. Keep your yarn neat and tidy. Make sure your needles stay paired together. Do not lose all your stitch markers or yarn needles at the bottom of a bag or drawer. By this point, you know what your favorite needles and supplies are. Clean out the "junk" that you did not like and proudly store those that you go to over and over again. If your supplies are easy to reach and well stored, you can get to them easily when you need them and know that they are in good shape when you are ready to go. For your yarn, consider storing it by color and weight so you can grab what you need when you need it. As you add more to the mix, find a place for it in your system, getting rid of something that does not fit anymore.

Make the investment now

When you first started, you were told to not buy the pricey stuff. Keep away from the expensive yarns. Try the more moderately priced needles first. Only buy a few things that you need to start. Now, you can splurge a little bit. Investing in an interchangeable needle set is a good idea for the intermediate knitter (that is you, now!). Buy a storage container that is made for more experienced knitters. Purchase those little accessories that will make knitting even easier for you. There is a host of options out there. Because you can accomplish so much and give such meaningful presents now, it is time to fork over the cash for the heirloom-quality needles and pricey cashmere yarn. You put in the time, now enjoy the reward.

Find a community

If you did not do this when you were starting out, now is the time to do it. Find a group of knitters of all skill levels to work on your projects with. Making sure it is a mix of people means that you can help the beginners get better because teaching is sometimes the best way to learn. Ask questions to the more advanced knitters. Those more advanced knitters may not be much more advanced than you, but they could have tried a technique or mastered a skill you want to learn and can be a handy resource along your journey. Coming into a group with only one skill level may seem like a good support group, but it will be hard to grow without the opportunity to learn and teach. Try to find a community that provides both for you. Plus, you are sure to have some good laughs along the way at all the silly mess up's that are made in all projects.

Do not be afraid to fail

You have made it this far; do not let the fear of a stitch or project hold you back now. This is the time to enjoy the challenge, but know you have the safety net of beginner projects to fall back on. Is the basketweave stitch not working out for you? Keep trying to master it. If you have a gift to give, create the project with a stitch you know and then go back to practice the basketweave.

Try to read your stitches

A true intermediate knitter will read their knitting like a book. You can look at your project and name all the stitches and techniques you did on each row, reading the row like a line in a book. This skill is not only incredibly impressive, but it also lets you find mistakes and fix them quickly before it causes problems. As you keep practicing and repeating projects, you will become more and more familiar with the look of the stitch variations. It may seem impossible to identify this in the beginning, but by now, you should be getting kind of good at it. As you move through this intermediate stage, you will get even better. Before you know it, you might be reading your knitting to your kids as a bedtime story.

CHAPTER 10

How To Finish Your Knitted Pieces?

Once you have reached the end of your project, you may feel you can't wait to cast off, sew it together, and see how everything turned out. But instead of rushing it, this a good time to make sure your project is finished the way you want it to be done. For example, if you find that your knitting style is too tight, then you may want to switch to larger needles for the closing edge.

The blocking process, which is done by wetting or steaming the knitted pieces to even out the stitches, enables the fibers to adapt to the shape and mesh into position. While this blocking isn't always necessary for every project, most apparel will look better if you do this blocking. But if you are using fine yarns for knitting lace shawls, this locking into place makes the sewing process easier and gives your project a professional finish. To block a piece, you have to put it on a flat surface larger than the larger knitted piece, such as your kitchen counter or your kitchen table. Or you can create a blocking table by taking a panel of wood or other stiff material and wrapping it with padding, such as foam, and then covering that with a towel and then adding another layer of toweling or thick material and staple everything to the board.

With natural fibers such as cotton, wool, cotton, cashmere, linen, and alpaca, the steam pressing wet blocking method works. But for blended yarns, such blended wools, mohair, or synthetics, which don't do well with wetting, you should lay the piece on a blocking surface without pinning it down and dampen it thoroughly with a fine spray mist. Then pin the piece with long pins. Start with pinning the length, then the width. Do the corners and any curved areas last. Measure the dimensions against those in the pattern. Use as many pins as possible to ensure that your piece is of the correct size. Let the piece dry on the block. However, if you have ribbed areas that are meant to stretch back into shape, don't block those areas, or the elasticity will be reduced.

Putting it together: Sewing

Sewing is probably considered the most unpleasant part of knitting. It can be tedious to make sure the right sides and the sides of the right sides are equal but paying extra attention to these details with making your project a success. There are two main stitches in sewing your pieces, the backstitch, and the mattress stitch. The backstitch provides strong stitching ideal for horizontal and curved seams, such as around holes and along the shoulders. The mattress knit is used for side seams and seams that don't require a lot of elasticity. Locking the pieces together properly can be a much easier task if you use a good many pins, and as you pin, ease the fullness with your fingers so that the pieces match.

With a standard sweater or cardigan, you will usually sew one or both of the shoulder seams, work in the neck area, sew the sleeves in place, and end up by sewing the side and sleeve seams. Use the same yarn that you used for knitting the garment, or if you have a multi-colored project, pick the most dominant color and match it with a plain yarn. Secure the thread by working a couple of back stitches near the edge of the seam, then work your way through the seam with your desired stitch, pulling the thread firmly but not enough to pucker the seam. Of course, as you work, you will need to keep checking the correct side of the piece to make sure you don't have any loose yarn loops sticking out.

The last step is to press the seams together. Either of these methods will do the job:

1. Take a clean, moist towel over the seams and press open with an iron on low heat by lifting the iron on and off the seam. Do not use a sliding motion.
2. Moisten the seam with spray around the inside of the piece and press it open to flatten and let it dry.

Double Mounted (needle)

1. Place the needle under the left armpit, take with the right hand the thread with which you have to work (colored in orange for better identification), leaving on the left a piece of thread 3 times longer than the width of the work (colored in yellow). Roll the part of the orange thread between the thumb and the index of the right hand.

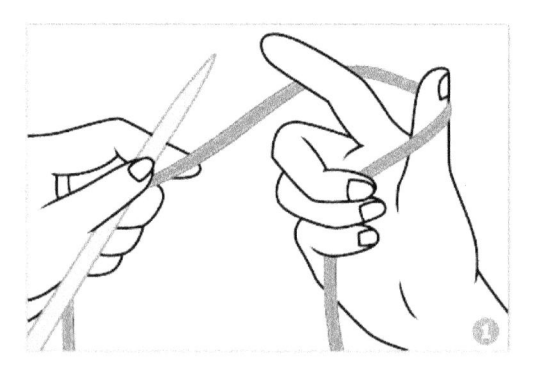

2. Return the hand a little while folding the index so that a loop is formed around it.

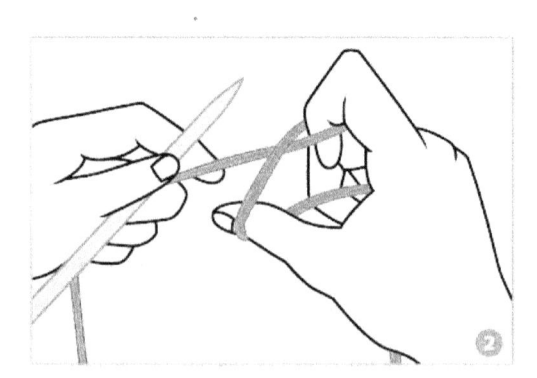

3. Explanations 1 and 2 are a suggestion of how to make the loop; you can vary the method as long as the result is the same. Then the steps to follow must be done to the letter. Insert the needle into the loop. Keeping the index finger inside this loop is optional.

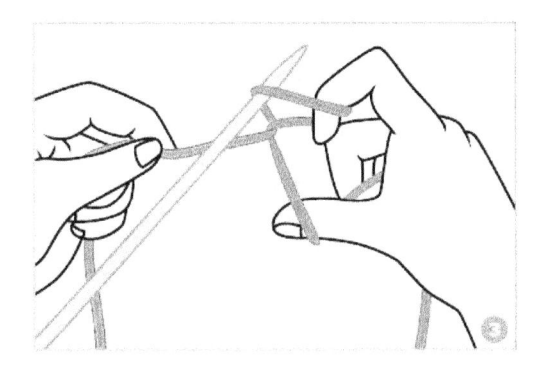

4. First, make a loop (yellow sector) with the strand of the ball in front of the orange loop and then pass this loop over the yellow loop until it is removed from the needle and release.

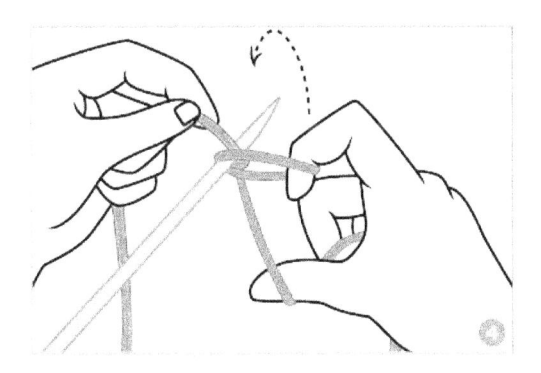

5. Hold the left-hand thread to adjust the point a little (orange sector). This first mounting point is usually a little loose and is reinforced by mounting the next point. If you prefer, you can mount the first point by making a sliding knot. Redo a loop as in the first step repeating the process until the necessary number of points is made.

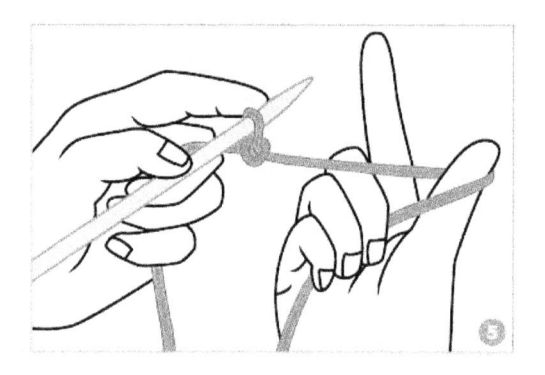

CONCLUSION

Thank you for making it to the end. Despite the fact that you might need to hop directly in there and begin utilizing a knitting pattern, it is a smart thought to make a check swatch. Try not to skirt this progression, you will be grieved, and it's not justified, despite any potential benefits. A large portion of a line in one inch can wind up having a major effect on the general size of a sweater. Continuously weave the swatch in the join that you will utilize. Clearly, different knitting patterns end up with different sizes, so this issue. I generally attempt to make my swatch sufficiently large to make it a decent test. I generally go for at any rate 4" x 4". Encompass the swatch with a couple of columns of seed fasten knitting (weave or purl the contrary line of what you see confronting you on odd number lines). Start and end each line with four seed lines also. This join lies an exceptionally level and will assist you with estimating precisely.

Needle size is substantially less significant than the strain with a knitting pattern. A few people are free with their knitting patterns, while others are tight. You can purposely adjust your pressure to make a different knitting pattern look. Free for a light open feel and more tightly for a hotter vibe. The more tightly weave may feel stiffer while the looser knitting piece may feel milder.

At the point when you have completed, the swatch let it sit for a spell. The yarn needs to unwind and level out any difficult situations. Presently check the fastens and measure the columns per inch with a material tape. Make sure to attempt an estimation in a couple of different spots. Another route is to simply ascertain how enormous the all-out knitting pattern swatch ought to be. If 16 joins were thrown on for the and the check is 4th=1," the swatch should quantify 4" (don't gauge the seed fastens on each end). If you are excessively enormous, attempt needles that are a size littler. Or then again, if you are excessively little, attempt bigger needles. Presently you have completed. You can begin your knitting pattern with certainty, realizing that the result of your works will really fit you!

I believe you have had a nice time going through all this. Knitting is a great hobby/occupation. As you begin your knitting journey, you will realize that your knitting is lose and sloppy, not to worry, though, because you will get better with time. All you need to do is to practice, practice, and practice some more until you become a guru at knitting.

If you are chasing a pattern or two, you will find that there are plenty of free ones online, and if you require a little extra tuition to improve your knitting techniques, you might also like to browse YouTube for additional knitting tutorials.

Now you know what you're doing and what you need to do to get started and continue. It's all about practice, and you need to take a break every now and again. Stretch your fingers, as it'll help to make sure that you don't' make simple mistakes that will cause you to get frustrated and put the knitting down. Knitting may be a hobby, but it's one that does take time.

CPSIA information can be obtained
at www.ICGtesting.com
Printed in the USA
LVHW021326230121
677173LV00005B/519